LITERARY PRIZES
AND THEIR WINNERS

LITERARY PRIZES
AND THEIR WINNERS

1946
R. R. BOWKER CO.
New York

807.9
LIT

542111

PRINTED AND BOUND IN THE UNITED STATES OF AMERICA
BY THE NEWPORT PRINTING CORPORATION

PREFACE

A book that wins a prize wins readers. Awards given to books make people more ready to read those books, for the winning of a literary prize is a piece of news which helps lift that volume above the common level and catches the attention of a whole new public. Thus the selling power of a book is instantly increased when it becomes a prize winner. This distinction prolongs its sale and often stays by it into old age. Prizes help to sell "old" books as well as "new," and keep the books of yesterday still in demand today.

Literary prizes have become so numerous that some guide is needed to their winners and this volume, now in its third revision, is intended to put into easily available form the constantly sought records of the books and authors which have won distinction in this way. The established annual prizes of many countries are included, such as the Nobel, Goncourt, Pulitzer, Hawthornden, James Tait Black, Newbery, Caldecott, as well as many unique and unrepeated prizes. The information in regard to Continental prizes is not as complete as might be desired, but it is the latest word that could be obtained under the stress of the times.

As literary prizes have developed in the United States, they fall into three general classifications—annual awards, with monetary or honorary recognition (or both) ; fellowships for literary work in progress ; and prize contests, some of which are established on an annual or semi-annual basis. The list of publishers' prize contests is constantly expanding, as this method of finding new talent has proved successful. Recently some of the large motion picture companies have adopted prize novel competitions with large money awards as a means of obtaining new film story material.

Some drama awards are included in this volume, although it is not within its scope to be all-inclusive in this field. Journalism awards for the most part are omitted. Only the important short story competitions conducted in cooperation with book publishers have been covered.

LITERARY PRIZES

Every effort has been made to make the listings as inclusive as possible. However, because of necessary limitations of space, in some few cases winners of awards prior to 1939 are not included in this edition. In all such instances users of the volume are referred to the 1939 edition of *Famous Literary Prizes and Their Winners* for the names of prize winners up to that date.

It is not possible to devise a wholly satisfactory way of listing the dates of the awards. The best plan seems to be to give the year in which the award was announced. Most annual awards are for the books of the previous calendar year, although some prizes are offered in recognition of a life's work. Unless otherwise noted it may be assumed that the date of the inauguration of the various awards is that of the first prize winner given.

No attempt has been made to ascertain whether or not the titles listed are now in print. They have been included with the name of the original publisher. In the case of awards made outside of the United States, the American publisher is given when known; otherwise, the original publisher's name appears.

The first two editions of this book, which appeared in 1935 and 1939, were edited by Miss Bessie Graham, of Philadelphia, compiler of the well-known reference book, *The Bookman's Manual* (Bowker). However, with this third edition, the task of revision has been assumed by the publisher's staff. To all those who have assisted on this volume, the editor is most grateful, but particularly to Ruth Ellen Bains, who has seen the book through to its completion. We will be glad to receive word of corrections and omissions, and of new prizes which may be established.

Anne J. Richter

New York, N. Y.
October 1946

CONTENTS

NOBEL PRIZE

Nobel Prize for Literature

Of all the literary prizes, the Nobel Prize for Literature is the highest in value and in honor bestowed. It is one of the five prizes founded by Alfred Bernhard Nobel (1833-1896), the other four awards being for Physics, Chemistry, Medicine and Peace. It consists of a medal in gold bearing an inscription suitable to the recipient, and a sum of money which originally amounted to $40,000. This sum has fluctuated over the years. In 1946 it amounted to $33,700. In 1946 the Swedish Parliament voted to exempt the Nobel Foundation from all taxation. Therefore, effective in 1948, $10,000 will be added to each Nobel Prize.

The Nobel Prize for Literature is awarded by the Swedish Academy in Stockholm. The official announcement is made on the tenth of December, the anniversary of Nobel's death. Because of the war, no awards were made between 1939 and 1944.

Alfred Nobel was a Swede who amassed a fortune of seventy million dollars from the manufacture of dynamite, an invention which he had made and patented in Europe, England and America. He began his career by manufacturing nitroglycerine in a factory in Sweden. An explosion caused the death of his brother, Oscar, and the crippling of his father. From this disaster came Nobel's determination to find a less dangerous substance and his efforts resulted in his discovery of dynamite. He maintained a factory in Sweden, another in California, and the largest dynamite factory in the world at Aberdeen, Scotland.

By the terms of Nobel's will the prize for literature is to be given to "the person who shall have produced in the field of literature the most distinguished work of an idealistic tendency."

Although the prize would seem, from a reading of Nobel's will, to have been intended for the encouragement of the struggling author and as an incentive to future work rather than a reward for past work, the Academy has rarely so awarded it. The Nobel Prize is not awarded to any particular book, but rather to an author for the sum total of his works. No one may apply for the Nobel Prize; it is not for competition.

Three times an American has won the Nobel Prize for Literature and in medicine, physics and peace, the honor has come to America repeatedly. During the war years there were no less than twenty-eight Nobel Prize winner living in the United States, including such distinguished literary figures as Sigrid Undset, Thomas Mann and Maurice Maeterlinck.

LITERARY PRIZES

NOBEL PRIZE WINNERS IN LITERATURE

Although this prize is awarded on the basis of the author's complete work, his outstanding books are given herewith.

1901 Sully Prudhomme. French poet. A few of his poems translated by Dante Gabriel Rossetti. (Oxford.)

1902 Theodor Mommsen. German historian. *History of Rome.* 4 vols. (Dutton.)

1903 Björnstjerne Björnson. Norwegian dramatist, poet and novelist. *Plays, First and Second Series.* (Scribner.)

1904 Frédéric Mistral. Provençal poet and philologist. *Mirèio,* a pastoral epic, translated by Harriet W. Preston. (Roberts Brothers.) José Echegaray. Spanish dramatist. *Always Ridiculous, Madman or Saint.* (Bruce Humphries.)

1905 Henryk Sienkiewicz. Polish novelist. *Quo Vadis?* (Little.)

1906 Giosuè Carducci. Italian poet. *Selections and Translations* by G. L. Bickersteth. (Longmans.)

1907 Rudyard Kipling. English novelist and poet. *Complete Works.* (Doubleday.)

1908 Rudolf Eucken. German philosopher. *The Meaning and Value of Life.* (Macmillan.)

1909 Selma Lagerlöf. Swedish novelist and poet. *The Wonderful Adventures of Nils; The Story of Gösta Berling; Märbacka.* (Doubleday.)

1910 Paul Heyse. German novelist, lyricist, and dramatist. *L'Arrabbiata.* (Translation Publishing Co.)

1911 Maurice Maeterlinck. Belgian dramatist. *Works.* (Dodd.)

1912 Gerhart Hauptmann. German dramatist and novelist. *Dramatic Works,* 9 vols. (Viking.)

1913 Rabindranath Tagore. East Indian essayist and poet. *Sadhana; Gitanjali.* (Macmillan.)

1914 No award.

1915 Romain Rolland. French novelist. *Jean-Christophe.* (Holt.)

1916 Verner von Heidenstam. Sweden's Poet Laureate. *Sweden's Laureate: Selected Poems,* translated by Charles Wharton Stork. (Yale.)

1917 Karl Gjellerup. Danish novelist and poet. Erik Pontoppidan. Danish novelist.

1918 No award.

1919 Carl Spitteler. Swiss novelist and poet. *Selected Poems.* (Putnam.) *Prometheus and Epimetheus.* (Scribner.)

1920 Knut Hamsun. Norwegian novelist. *Growth of the Soil.* (Knopf.) *Hunger.* (Knopf.)

1921 Anatole France. French novelist. *Works.* (Dodd.)

1922 Jacinto Benavente. Spanish dramatist. *Plays.* (Scribner.)

1923 William Butler Yeats. Irish poet. *Selected Poems.* (Macmillan.)

1924 Ladislaw Stanislaw Reymont. Polish novelist. *The Peasants.* 4 vols. (Knopf.)

1925 George Bernard Shaw. Irish dramatist. *Works.* (Dodd.)

1926 Grazia Deledda. Italian novelist. *The Mother.* (Macmillan.)

1927   Henri Louis Bergson. French philosopher. *Creative Evolution.* (Holt.)
1928   Sigrid Undset. Norwegian novelist. *Kristin Lavransdatter* (trilogy); *The Master of Hestviken* (tetralogy). (Knopf.)
1929   Thomas Mann. German novelist. *Buddenbrooks; The Magic Mountain; Joseph and His Brothers.* (Knopf.)
1930   Sinclair Lewis. American novelist. *Main Street; Babbitt; Arrowsmith.* (Harcourt.)
1931   Erik Axel Karlfeldt. Swedish lyric poet. (Awarded posthumously.) Karlfeldt had refused the award ten years before on the grounds that he was not read outside of Sweden.
1932   John Galsworthy. English novelist and dramatist. *Works.* (Scribner.)
1933   Ivan Alexeyevich Bunin. Russian novelist and dramatist. *The Well of Days; The Village; The Gentleman from San Francisco.* (Knopf.)
1934   Luigi Pirandello. Italian novelist and dramatist. *As You Desire Me; The Outcast; Tonight We Improvise.* (Dutton.)
1935   No award.
1936   Eugene O'Neill. American dramatist. *Works.* (Random.)
1937   Roger Martin du Gard. French novelist. *The Thibaults.* (Viking.)
1938   Pearl S. Buck. American novelist. *The Good Earth.* (John Day.)
1939   Frans Eemil Sillanpää. Finnish novelist. *Meek Heritage.* (Knopf.) *The Maid Silja.* (Macmillan.)
1940 - 1943   No awards.
1944   Johannes V. Jensen. Danish novelist and poet. *The Long Journey.* (Knopf.)
1945   Gabriela Mistral (Lucila Godoy y Alcayaga). Chilean poet. *Desolacion.* (Instituto de las Espanas en los Estados Unidos of Columbia University.)
1946   Hermann Hesse. German-Swiss novelist, poet and essayist. *Death and the Lover* (Dodd); *Steppenwolf* (Holt.)

AMERICAN PRIZES

GENERAL PRIZES

American Academy of Arts and Letters
National Institute of Arts and Letters

The National Institute of Arts and Letters, at 633 West 155th Street, New York 32, was organized at a meeting of the American Social Science Association in 1898. Membership was at first restricted to one hundred and fifty, but was later increased to two hundred and fifty. Eligibility for membership is conditioned upon distinguished attainment in literature or the fine arts. The American Academy of Arts and Letters was organized in 1904. Its membership is limited to fifty. The American Academy is a smaller group within the National Institute of Arts and Letters In order to become eligible to the American Academy one must first be a member of the National Institute. In addition to the literary awards listed below, the American Academy and the National Institute award prizes in other branches of the arts.

AWARD OF MERIT MEDAL

The American Academy Award of Merit is a $1,000 prize accompanied by a medal. It is presented to an outstanding person in America representing one of the following arts: painting, sculpture, novel, poetry, drama. This award, established in 1942, is made in one of these fields each year, in the order given above, but is never made to any member of the Academy or of the National Institute.

1942 Charles Burchfield (painting.)
1943 Carl Wilhelm Milles (sculpture.)
1944 Theodore Dreiser (novel.)
1945 Wystan Hugh Auden (poetry.)
1946 John van Druten (drama.)

AMERICAN ACADEMY OF ARTS AND LETTERS GOLD MEDAL

The Gold Medal of the American Academy is conferred in recognition of special distinction in literature, art or music. It is given for the entire work of the recipient who must be a native or naturalized citizen of the United States. The Medal, which was designed by James Earle Fraser, is always given to non-members.

The winners of the medal from 1915 to 1930 may be found in the 1939 edition of *Famous Literary Prizes and Their Winners*. No Medal was awarded between 1930 and 1942.

1942 Ernest Bloch (Music.)

LITERARY PRIZES

WILLIAM DEAN HOWELLS MEDAL

The Howells Medal of the American Academy is, as stated by the donor, "to commemorate the name of our great American novelist." It is awarded every fifth year in recognition of the most distinguished work of American fiction published during that period. The funds necessary to provide this gold medal, designed by Anna Hyatt Huntington, were accepted by the Academy in 1921 on the eighty-fourth anniversary of the birth of William Dean Howells. The first award was made in 1925.

1925 Mary E. Wilkins Freeman, for her entire work.
1930 Willa Cather, for *Death Comes for the Archbishop*. (Knopf.)
1935 Pearl Buck, for *The Good Earth*. (John Day.)
1940 Ellen Glasgow, for her entire work.
1945 Booth Tarkington, for fiction.

AWARD FOR DISTINGUISHED ACHIEVEMENT

In 1945 the National Institute created the Award for Distinguished Achievement, providing a prize of $1,000. It is to be given to an eminent foreign artist, composer or writer living in America.

1945 Richard Beer-Hofmann, Austrian.
1946 Ralph Hodgson, English.

NATIONAL INSTITUTE FELLOWSHIPS

In 1945 two fellowships were established in memory of Edwin Arlington Robinson and Edward MacDowell. The first awards under this endowment were made in 1946.

1946 Edwin Arlington Robinson Fellowship—Edward Trask, writer.
Edward MacDowell Fellowship—Hans Sahl, writer, and Robert E. Strassburg, composer. (Divided award.)

NATIONAL INSTITUTE GOLD MEDAL

The Gold Medal of the Institute is awarded annually to any citizen of the United States for distinguished services to arts or letters in the creation of original work. Awards have been made for sculpture, history, poetry, architecture, drama, painting, fiction, essays, biography, and music. Recipients of the Gold Medal for the years before 1935 may be found in the 1939 edition of *Famous Literary Prizes and Their Winners*.

1935 Agnes Repplier (essays and belles-lettres.)
1936 George Gray Barnard (sculpture.)
1937 Charles McLean Andrews (history and biography.)

1938   Walter Damrosch (music.)
1939   Robert Frost (poetry.)
1940   William Adams Delano (architecture.)
1941   Robert E. Sherwood (drama.)
1942. Cecilia Beaux (painting.)
1943   Stephen Vincent Benét (literature.)
1944   Willa Cather (fiction.)
1945   Paul Manship (sculpture.)
1946   Van Wyck Brooks (essays and criticism.)

AMERICAN ACADEMY AND NATIONAL INSTITUTE GRANTS

In 1940 the American Academy and the National Institute of Arts and Letters established Grants to be awarded to non-members. The Grants were $500 when first given in 1941; in 1942 they were increased to $1,000. The awards are "to aid in furthering creative work by American artists and to honor them for past achievement with a practical recognition." The recipients for literature have been:

1941   Mary M. Colum
      Jesse Stuart
1942   Hermann Broch
      Norman Corwin
      Edgar Lee Masters
      Muriel Rukeyser
1943   Virgil Geddes
      Carson McCullers
      José Garcia Villa
      Joseph Wittlin
1944   Hugo Ignotus
      Jeremy Ingalls
      Thomas Sancton
      Karl Jay Shapiro
      Eudora Welty
      Tennessee Williams

1945   Kenneth Fearing
      Feike Feikema
      Alexander Greendale
      Norman Rosten
      Jean Stafford
      Marguerite Young
1946   Gwendolyn Brooks
      Kenneth Burke
      Malcolm Cowley
      Peter de Vries
      Langston Hughes
      Arthur Laurents
      Marianne Moore
      Arthur Schlesinger, Jr.
      Irwin Shaw

RUSSELL LOINES MEMORIAL FUND

In 1924 the friends of Russell Loines, desiring to perpetuate his memory, established, and asked the National Institute of Arts and Letters to administer, a fund to be known as the Russell Loines Memorial Fund, the income from which is to be given periodically to some American or English poet not as a prize, but as a recognition of value. The sum was approximately $9,000, and the council, believing that awards of $1,000 should be made, wait until the accumulated income reaches that sum.

1931 *Collected Poems of Robert Frost,* by Robert Frost. (Holt.)
1933 *The Boar and the Shibboleth,* by Edward Doro. (Knopf.)
1939 *Letter to a Comrade,* by Joy Davidman. (Yale.)
1942 *Poems: 1930-1940,* by Horace Gregory. (Harcourt.)

The A. B. A. National Book Awards

During the seven years from 1936 through 1942 the American Booksellers Association, 35 East 20th St., New York 3, gave National Book Awards at the time of their annual convention. The award took the form of an engraved bronze paperweight. The selections were made by a vote of booksellers throughout the the country from a list compiled by a special committee of the A. B. A. There were five possible awards—the most distinguished novel of the year; the most distinguished non-fiction of the year; the most distinguished biography of the year; the most original book of the year; the forgotten book of the year—but awards were not always made for each category. During the war years when no A. B. A. conventions were held, the awards were discontinued and have not been resumed.

1936 *Time Out of Mind,* by Rachel Field. (Macmillan.) Fiction.
North to the Orient, by Anne Lindbergh. (Harcourt.) Non-fiction.
Personal History, by Vincent Sheean. (Doubleday.) Biography.
Circus of Dr. Lao, by Charles G. Finney. (Viking.) Original book.

1937 *Gone with the Wind,* by Margaret Mitchell. (Macmillan.) Fiction.
The Flowering of New England, by Van Wyck Brooks. (Dutton.) Non-fiction.
An American Doctor's Odyssey, by Victor Heiser. (Norton.) Biography.
The Country Kitchen, by Delia T. Lutes. (Little.) Original book.
I Met a Gypsy, by Nora Lofts. (Knopf.) Forgotten book.

1938 *The Citadel,* by A. J. Cronin. (Little.) Fiction.
Madame Curie, by Eve Curie. (Doubleday.) Non-fiction and Biography.
400,000,000 Customers, by Carl Crow. (Harper.) Original book.
On Borrowed Time, by Lawrence Watkins. (Knopf.) Forgotten book.

1939 *Rebecca,* by Daphne du Maurier. (Doubleday.) Fiction.
      Listen! the Wind, by Anne Morrow Lindbergh. (Harcourt.) Non-fiction.
      With Malice Toward Some, by Margaret Halsey. (Simon & Schuster.) Original book.
      The World Was My Garden, by David Fairchild. (Scribner.) Forgotten book.

1940 *The Grapes of Wrath,* by John Steinbeck. (Viking.) Fiction.
      Wind, Sand and Stars, by Antoine de Saint Exupéry. (Reynal). Non-fiction.
      Johnny Got His Gun, by Dalton Trumbo. (Lippincott.) Original book.
      Ararat, by Elgin Groseclose. (Carrick.) Booksellers' discovery.

1941 *How Green Was My Valley,* by Richard Llewellyn. (Macmillan.) Fiction.
      As I Remember Him, by Hans Zinsser. (Little.) Non-fiction.
      Who Walk Alone, by Perry Burgess. (Holt.) Booksellers' discovery.

1942 *Hold Autumn in Your Hand,* by George Sessions Perry. (Viking.) Booksellers' discovery.

The American Historical Association Prizes

The American Historical Association awards are designed particularly to encourage those who have not published previously any considerable work nor established a wide reputation. All works submitted in competition for these prizes must be in the hands of the prize committee on or before the first of June in the year in which the award is made. The date of publication of printed monographs submitted in competition must fall within a period of two and one-half years prior to June first of the year of the award. Further information concerning the prizes may be obtained from the American Historical Association, Library of Congress Annex, Washington 25, D. C.

HERBERT BAXTER ADAMS PRIZE

The Herbert Baxter Adams Prize, without stipend, is awarded in even-numbered years for a monograph, in manuscript or in print, in the field of European history.

1938 *French Foreign Policy During the Administration of Cardinal Fleury, 1726-1743,* by Arthur McCandless Wilson. (Harvard Univ. Press.)

LITERARY PRIZES

1940 *Church and State in Russia, 1900-1917,* by John Shelton Curtiss. (Columbia Univ. Press.)

1942 *Rival Ambassadors at the Court of Queen Mary,* by E. Harris Harbison. (Princeton Univ. Press.)

1944 *The Russian Fur Trade,* 1550-1700, by R. H. Fisher. (Univ. of Calif. Press.)

GEORGE LOUIS BEER PRIZE

The George Louis Beer Prize of about $200 is awarded annually for the best work on any phase of European international history since 1895. Competition is limited to citizens of the United States and to works in the English language actually submitted. A work may be submitted either in manuscript or in print. Previous winners of this award may be found in the 1939 edition of *Famous Literary Prizes and Their Winners.*

1939 *Background of Anti-English Feeling in Germany, 1890-1902,* by Pauline Relyea Anderson. (American Univ. Press.)

1940 *The American Impact on Great Britain, 1898-1914,* by Richard Heathcote Heindel. (Univ. of Pennsylvania Press.)

1941 *The Anatomy of British Sea Power,* by Arthur J. Marder. (Knopf.)

1942 No award.

1943 *British Enterprise in Nigeria,* by Arthur Norton Cook. (Univ. of Pennsylvania Press.)

1944 No award.

1945 No award.

ALBERT J. BEVERIDGE MEMORIAL PRIZE

The Albert J. Beveridge Memorial Prize of $200 is awarded biennially in odd-numbered years for a monograph, in manuscript or in print, in the field of the history of the Western Hemisphere. (This award has taken the place of the Justin Winsor Prize, previously awarded.)

1939 *James Kent: A Study in Conservatism,* by John T. Horton. (Appleton.)

1941 *The Background of the Revolution in Maryland,* by Charles A. Barker. (Yale Univ. Press.)

1943 *The American Frontier in Hawaii: The Pioneers, 1789-1843,* by Harold Whitman Bradley. (Stanford Univ. Press.)

1945 *John Stuart and the Southern Colonial Frontier,* by John Richard Alden. (Univ. of Mich.)

AMERICAN PRIZES

JOHN H. DUNNING PRIZE

The John H. Dunning Prize of about $100 is awarded biennially in even-numbered years for the best work, either in print or in manuscript, on any subject relating to American history. Competition is limited to members of the American Historical Association. Previous winners of this award can be found in the 1939 edition of *Famous Literary Prizes and Their Winners.*

1940   *Robert Dale Owen,* by Richard W. Leopold (Harvard Univ. Press.)
1942   *Boston's Immigrants,* by Oscar Handlin. (Harvard Univ. Press.)
1944   *Admiral Sims and the Modern American Navy,* by Lt. Elting E. Morison, USNR. (Houghton.)

THE WATUMULL FOUNDATION TRIENNIAL PRIZE

The Watumull Foundation has established a prize of $500 to be awarded triennially by the American Historical Association to the author of the best book originally published in the United States on any phase of the history of India. The first award was announced at the annual meeting of the Association in December 1945. Books which publishers wish to submit should be sent to the committee on the Watumull Prize, American Historical Association, Room 614, Fayerweather Hall, Columbia University, New York 27, N. Y.

1945   *Chanhu-Daro Excavations, 1935-36,* by Ernest J. H. Mackay. (American Oriental Society.)

MEMORIAL FELLOWSHIP

A memorial fellowship of $1,000 has been established by the American Historical Association in honor of Albert J. Beveridge. It is to be awarded annually for the best original manuscript, either complete or in progress, on the history of the United States, Latin America, or Canada. The first award will be made in December of 1946.

This new fellowship represents an extension of the earlier program for the use of the Albert J. Beveridge fund.

Anisfield-Wolf Awards

The *Saturday Review of Literature* announced in 1934 a prize established by Mrs. Edith Anisfield Wolf of Cleveland, Ohio, in memory of her father, to be called the John Anisfield Award. The award was originally $1,000, but was later increased to $2,000 to provide for a second prize in the field of creative literature.

The name was changed to the Anisfield-Wolf Awards. The prizes are awarded annually for sound and significant books published in the United States or abroad on the subject of racial relations in the contemporary world. The prize is administered by a committee consisting of Henry Seidel Canby of the *Saturday Review of Literature*, Henry Pratt Fairchild of New York University, and Ralph Linton of Columbia University.

1935 *Negro Politicians: The Rise of Negro Politics in Chicago*, by Harold Foote Gosnell. (Univ. of Chicago Press.)

1936 *We Europeans: A Survey of Racial Problems*, by A. M. Carr-Saunders, Julian Huxley and A. C. Haddon. (Harper.)

1937 *We Americans: A Study of Cleavage in an American City*, by Elin L. Anderson. (Harvard Univ. Press.)

1938 *The Negro College Graduate*, by Charles S. Johnson. (Univ. of N. C. Press.)

1940 *The Negro Family in the United States*, by E. Franklin Frazier. (Univ. of Chicago Press.)

1941 *From Many Lands*, by Louis Adamic. (Harper.)

1942 *The Haitian People*, by James G. Leyburn. (Yale Univ. Press.) *Quest*, by Leopold Infeld. (Doubleday.)

1943 *Negroes in Brazil*, by Donald Pierson. (Univ. of Chicago Press.) *Dust Tracks on a Road*, by Zora Neale Hurston. (Lippincott.)

1944 *The World of Sholom Aleichem*, by Maurice Samuel. (Knopf.) *New World A-Coming*, by Roi Ottley. (Houghton.)

1945 *An American Dilemma: The Negro Problem and Modern Democracy*, by Gunnar Myrdal. (Harper.) *Earth and High Heaven*, by Gwethalyn Graham. (Lippincott.)

1946 *One Nation*, by Wallace Stegner & the editors of *Look*. (Houghton.) *Black Metropolis*, by St. Clair Drake and Horace R. Clayton. (Harcourt.)

Bross Foundation Prize

The trustees of Lake Forest College, Lake Forest, Illinois, offer a cash prize of $15,000 for the best book or manuscript, heretofore unpublished, on the connection, relation, and mutual bearing of the Humanities, the Social Sciences, the Biological Sciences, or any other branch of knowledge with and upon the Christian religion. The award was made in 1940 and is scheduled to be made again in 1950. The Bross Foundation was planned by William Bross in the years following the death of his infant son, Nattie, in 1856. Further information may be had by addressing the President of Lake Forest College.

1940 *Christianity: An Inquiry Into Its Nature and Truth*, by Harris Franklin Rall. (Scribner.)

AMERICAN PRIZES

The John Burroughs Medal

The bronze medal of the John Burroughs Association is awarded annually for "a foremost literary work in the field so eminently occupied during his lifetime by John Burroughs," who called himself a "literary naturalist." Books eligible for consideration should combine literary quality with accuracy of statement and should be based on originality of observations and conclusions. There is no restriction with regard to the place of publication but the book should be in English and should have been published within three years prior to the date of the award. This is not an open competition; the selection is made by the judges from books in print. Information concerning the award may be obtained from the John Burroughs Association, the American Museum of Natural History, Central Park West at 79th Street, New York 24, N. Y.

1926	William Beebe	1937	No award
1927	Ernest Thompson Seton	1938	Robert Cushman Murphy
1928	John Russell McCarthy	1939	T. Gilbert Pearson
1929	Frank M. Chapman	1940	Arthur Cleveland Bent
1930	Archibald Rutledge	1941	Louis J. Halle, Jr.
1931	No award	1942	Edward Allworthy
1932	Frederick S. Dellenbaugh		Armstrong
1933	Oliver P. Medsger	1943	Edwin Way Teale
1934	W. W. Christman	1944	No award
1935	No award	1945	Rutherford Platt
1936	Charles Crawford Gorst	1946	Francis Lee and Florence Page Jaques

California Medals

The Commonwealth Club of California annually awards two gold medals (one, the General Literature Gold Medal and the other, the Scholarship and Research Gold Medal) and several silver medals for the finest books by California authors published during the preceding year. Both fiction and non-fiction books on any subject are eligible for consideration. Entrants are not restricted to California themes. Further information may be obtained from the Literature Medal Award Jury, Commonwealth Club of California, Hotel St. Francis, San Francisco 19, California. Medal winners for the years 1931-1939 are listed in the 1939 edition of *Famous Literary Prizes and Their Winners.*

1940 *Grapes of Wrath,* by John Steinbeck. (Viking.) General Literature Gold Medal.

San Francisco's Literary Frontier, by Franklin Walker. (Knopf.) Scholarship and Research Gold Medal.

Flowering Earth, by Donald Culross Peattie. (Putnam.) Silver Medal.

Land Below the Wind, by Agnes Newton Keith. (Little.) Silver Medal.

The Time of Your Life, by William Saroyan. (Harcourt.) Silver Medal.

Death Loses a Pair of Wings, by Robin Lampson. (Scribner.) Poetry Silver Medal.

Bright Heritage, by Mary Virginia Provines. (Longmans.) Juvenile Silver Medal.

1941   *Wild Geese Calling,* by Stewart Edward White. (Doubleday.) General Literature Gold Medal.

The Structure of Art, by Carl Thurston. (Univ. of Chicago Press.) Scholarship and Research Gold Medal.

The March of the Barbarians, by Harold Lamb. (Doubleday.) Silver Medal.

My Name Is Aram, by William Saroyan. (Harcourt.) Silver Medal.

A Diplomatic History of the American People, by Thomas A. Bailey. (Crofts.) Silver Medal.

In What Hour, by Kenneth Rexroth. (Macmillan.) Poetry Silver Medal.

Blue Willow, by Doris Gates. (Viking.) Juvenile Silver Medal.

1942   *Anybody's Gold,* by Joseph Henry Jackson. (Appleton.) General Literature Gold Medal.

Many Mexicos, by Lesley Byrd Simpson. (Putnam.) Scholarship and Research Gold Medal.

When the Living Strive, by Richard T. LaPiere. (Harper.) Silver Medal.

Thackeray, by John W. Dodds. (Oxford Univ. Press.) Silver Medal.

The Morning of America, by Frank J. Klingberg. (Appleton.) Silver Medal.

1943   *I Remember Christine,* by Oscar Lewis. (Knopf.) General Literature Gold Medal.

History of Historical Writing, by James Westfall Thompson. (Macmillan.) Scholarship and Research Gold Medal.

Lord of Alaska, by Hector Chevigny. (Viking.) Silver Medal.

Man Who Killed the Deer, by Frank Waters. (Farrar & Rinehart.) Silver Medal.

The Stranger, by Lillian Bos Ross. (Morrow.) Silver Medal.

Proud Riders, by H. L. Davis. (Harper.) Poetry Silver Medal.

Long Adventure, by Hildegarde Hawthorne. (Appleton.) Juvenile Silver Medal.

1944   *Trio,* by Dorothy Baker. (Houghton.) General Literature Gold Medal.

The Legacy of Nazism, by Frank Munk. (Macmillan.) Scholarship and Research Gold Medal.

Wide Is the Gate, by Upton Sinclair. (Viking.) Silver Medal.

The Day of Reckoning, by Max Radin. (Knopf.) Silver Medal.

Brothers Under the Skin, by Carey McWilliams. (Little.) Silver Medal.

Spurs for Antonia, by Katherine Wigmore Eyre. (Oxford.) Juvenile Silver Medal.

Napoleon III, by Albert Guerard. (Harvard.) Special award of distinguished merit Silver Medal.

1945 *One Day on Beetle Rock,* by Sally Carrighar. (Knopf.) Gold Medal.

Woodrow Wilson and the Lost Peace, by Thomas Bailey. (Macmillan.) Gold Medal.

Forward Observer, by Edwin V. Westrate. (Dutton.) Silver Medal.

Captain Retread, by Donald Hough. (Norton.) Silver Medal.

Caesar and Christ, by Will Durant. (Simon & Schuster.) Silver Medal.

Phoenix and the Tortoise, by Kenneth Rexroth. (New Directions.) Poetry Silver Medal.

Thunderbolt House, by Howard Pease. (Doubleday.) Juvenile Silver Medal.

1946 *A Lion Is in the Streets,* by Adria Locke Langley. (Whittlesey.) General Literature Gold Medal.

Charlotte and Emily, by Laura L. Hinkley. (Hastings.) Scholarship and Research Gold Medal.

Minor Heresies, by John J. Espey. (Knopf.) Silver Medal.

High Bonnet, by Idwal Jones. (Prentice-Hall.) Silver Medal.

South America Called Them, by Victor Wolfgang von Hagen. (Knopf.) Silver Medal.

The Singing Cave, by Margaret Leighton. (Houghton.) Juvenile Silver Medal.

Catholic Literary Award

This award has been given annually since 1941 for the most outstanding book published by a member of the Gallery of Living Catholic Authors. The award is usually made on the last Sunday in October, the Feast of Christ the King, and takes the form of an honorary scroll bearing the name of the author and the date of the award. Further details may be obtained from the Gallery of Living Catholic Authors, Webster Groves, Missouri.

1941 *Autobiography,* by Eric Gill. (Devin-Adair.)

1942 *A Companion to the Summa,* by Father Walter Farrell. (Sheed & Ward.)

1943 *Pageant of the Popes,* by John Farrow. (Sheed & Ward.)

1944 *St. Teresa of Avila,* by William Thomas Walsh. (Bruce.)

1945 *New Testament in English,* by Monsignor Ronald Knox. (Sheed & Ward.)

1946 *Brideshead Revisited,* by Evelyn Waugh. (Little.)

LITERARY PRIZES

Friends of American Writers Award

The Friends of American Writers Foundation is a group of 400 Chicago women who award a cash prize every year to an author who is either a resident of the Middle West or who has written a book, fiction or non-fiction, concerning the Middle West.

Between 1928 and 1938 prizes were offered by this group ranging between $100 and $500 and were awarded to nineteen authors, among whom were Carl Sandburg, Harriet Monroe, Vincent Sheean, Donald Culross Peattie, and John Gunther. The prize now amounts to $750.

Details concerning the award may be obtained from Mrs. W. J. Bargen, 922 North Sheridan Rd., Waukegan, Illinois.

1938 *They Came Like Swallows,* by William Maxwell. (Harper.)
1939 *Wind Without Rain,* by Herbert Krause. (Bobbs.)
1940 *Ararat,* by Elgin Groseclose. (Carrick.)
1941 *Delilah,* by Marcus Goodrich. (Farrar & Rinehart.)
       Special award to *Poetry: A Magazine of Verse*
1942 *West of Midnight,* by Paul Engle. (Random.)
1943 *In the Forests of the Night,* by Kennth S. Davis. (Houghton.)
1944 *Retreat from Rostov,* by Paul Hughes. (Random.)
1945 *Final Score,* by Warren Beck. (Knopf.)
1946 *Dark Medallion,* by Dorothy Langley. (Simon & Schuster.)

John Simon Guggenheim Memorial Fellowships

In order to improve the quality of education, and the practice of arts and professions in the United States, to foster research, and to provide for the cause of better international understanding, the late United States Senator, Simon Guggenheim, and his wife established in 1925 the John Simon Guggenheim Memorial Foundation in memory of a son who died in 1922.

Four million dollars were devoted to the establishment of this foundation which provides fellowships for research in any field of knowledge and for creative work in any of the fine arts. The endowment of the Foundation now totals $28,000,000.

All the income is devoted to providing opportunities for men and women of high ability to further their work. The Foundation's assistance is given to scholars and artists in the form of fellowships. The funds granted each fellow are designed to be adequate to his needs for the period of the fellowship, depending upon the needs of the work at hand. Men and women, married or unmarried, without distinction of race, color or creed, are eligible on equal terms. The fellows are allowed to carry on their work anywhere in the world. Under one of the fellowship plans, grants are made to citizens and permanent residents of the United States; under another plan, grants are made to citizens of thirteen Latin American countries.

In 1944, in addition to the usual awards, the Foundation appropriated $200,000 for Post-Service Fellowships to be awarded to young scholars and artists who have served the war effort in the Armed Forces or other governmental services.

The Guggenheim Fellowships are awarded in the fields of art, music, history, science, creative writing, philosophy, etc. However, the list below includes only those in creative writing and biography. Fellowship winners in these fields for the years from 1928 through 1939 may be found in the 1939 edition of *Famous Literary Prizes and Their Winners*. In normal cases the stipend will not exceed $2,500 a year. Further details may be obtained from the John Simon Guggenheim Foundation, 551 Fifth Avenue, New York 17, N. Y.

GUGGENHEIM FELLOWS

R. Fernando Alegría (1946) (Chile)
Wystan Hugh Auden (1942)
Dorothy Baker (1942)
Howard Baker (1944)
Jacques Barzun (1945)
Hermann J. Broch (1940 and 1941)
Gwendolyn Brooks (1946)
Henrietta Buckmaster (1944)
Marie Campbell (1944)
Wilbur J. Cash (1941)
Brainard Cheney (1941)
Edwin Corle (1941)
Reuel N. Denney (1941)
Ward Allison Dorrance (1940)
John Dos Passos (1940 and 1942)
Charles Warren Everett (1944)
Lloyd Frankenberg (1940)
Arturo Arnáiz y Freg (1942) (Mexico)
Lewis Galantière (1940)
Maxwell David Gesimar (1942)
Alexander Greendale (1942)

Jean Stafford Lowell (1945)
Andrew Nelson Lytle (1940 and 1941)
Hugh MacLennan (1943)
Carson McCullers (1942 and 1946)
Gustavus Meyers (1942)
Marianne Moore (1945)
Wigherto Jiménez Moreno (1942) (Mexico)
Wright Morris (1942)
Vladimir Nabokov (1943)
Justin O'Brien (1942)
Octavio Paz (1943)
Robert Pick (1945)
Frederick Pottle (1945)
Vladimir Pozner (1943)
Gordon Morton Ray (1942)
Jay Saunders Redding (1944)
Theodore Roethke (1945)
Kathleen Romoli (1943)
Norman Rosten (1941)
Muriel Rukeyser (1943)
Ralph Leslie Rusk (1945)
Mark Schorer (1941 and 1942)

LITERARY PRIZES

Alfred Whitney Griswold (1942)
Alrick Gustafson (1945)
Jeremy Ingalls (1943)
Randall Jarrell (1946)
Israel James Kapstein (1944)
Alfred Kazin (1940)
Marie Kimball (1945)
Oliver La Farge (1941)
Edwin Lanham (1940)
Gabriel Fernández Ledesma
  (1942) (Mexico)
Roger Lemelin (1946)
Antonio Hernández Travieso
  (1942 and 1943) (Cuba)
José Garcia Villa (1943)
Hugh Mason Wade (1943 and
  1944)
Dixon Wecter (1942)
Edward Weismiller (1943)

Delmore Schwartz (1940 and
  1941)
Ramón J. Sender (1941)
  (Mexico)
Madeleine B. Stern (1943 and
  1944)
Virginia Eggertsen Sorenson
  (1946)
Randall Stewart (1943)
James Still (1941 and 1946)
Laurence Thompson (1945)
Signe Kirstine Toksvig (1943)
Eudora Welty (1942)
Christine Weston (1940)
David Willson (1943)
Arthur Ramous Wilmurt (1946)
Howard Wolf (1940)
Morton Dauwen Zabel (1944)
George Zabriskie (1942 and 1946)

POST-SERVICE FELLOWSHIPS

Herbert Aptheker (1945)
John Bakeless (1945)
Ben Belitt (1945)
Sam Byrd (1946)
Hodding Carter (1945)
Paul G. Horgan (1945)
Everette Howard Hunt, Jr. (1946)
Adrienne Koch (1945)
Stanley Kunitz (1945)

Oliver La Farge (1945)
Jerre Mangione (1945)
Caroline Bache McMahon (1945)
Dale Morgan (1945)
James R. Newman (1946)
Karl Shapiro (1944)
Bradford Smith (1946)
William E. Wilson (1945)

The Avery Hopwood and Jule Hopwood Prizes

Since 1931 prizes for student writing have been awarded at the University of Michigan. These awards were made possible by Avery Hopwood, the dramatist, an alumnus of the university, who provided that prizes be given each year "to students who perform the best creative work in the fields of dramatic writing, fiction, poetry and the essay." Major and minor awards are made in each field and have varied from $75 to $2,500. Only regularly enrolled students in the University of Michigan may enter the competition. The list below includes only those winners whose books have been published since 1939. A partial list of winners from 1933 through 1938 appears in the earlier edition of *Famous Literary Prizes and Their Winners*. For further information, write to the University of Michigan, Ann Arbor, Michigan.

1939 *Homeward to America*, by John Anthony Ciardi. (Holt.)
The Loon Feather, by Iola Fuller. (Harcourt.)

1940 *Whistle Stop*, by Maritta Wolff. (Random.)
Lincoln Lyrics, by John Malcolm Brinnin. (New Directions.)

1941 *Nearer the Earth*, by Beatrice Borst. (Random.)

1942 *November Storm*, by Jay McCormick. (Doubleday.)
Golden Apples of the Sun, by Rosemary Obermeyer. (Dutton.)
Dancing Saints, by Ann George Leslie. (Doubleday.)
Rising Wind, by Sister Mary Edwardine. (Bruce Humphries.)

1943 *The Broken Pitcher*, by Naomi Gilpatrick. (Dial.)
Delay is the Song, by Rosamond Haas. (Dutton.)

1944 *A Sweep of Dusk*, by William Kehoe. (Dutton.)
Years Before the Flood, by Marianne Roane. (Scribner.)
34 Charlton Street, by Rene Kuhn. (Appleton.)
Family Tree, by Florence Maple. (Knopf.)

1945 *The Gifts of Love*, by Adrina Iverson. (Farrar, Straus, with Duell, Sloan & Pearce.)
Rip Van Winkle's Dream, by Jeannette Haien. (Doubleday.)
Clementine, by Peggy Goodin. (Dutton.)
By Their Fruits, by Julia Neal. (Univ. of N. C. Press.)

1946 *The Practicing of Christopher*, by Josephine Eckert. (Dial.)
No More With Me, by Russell M. LaDue, Jr. (Doubleday.)
The Grass Divides, by Kathleen Hughes Thumin. (Doubleday.)

Laetare Medal

The Laetare Medal has been awarded annually since 1883 by the Academic Council of the University of Notre Dame, Notre Dame, Indiana, as a recognition of merit and an incentive to greater achievement. The faith of the winner is not mentioned in the terms of the award, but the prize has always been given to a distinguished member of the Catholic laity. The name of the recipient is announced on Laetare Sunday, the fourth Sunday in Lent.

The list below includes only those winners since 1937 who have received the award for literary work.

1941 William Thomas Walsh, journalist and author.
1942 Helen Constance White, author and teacher.
1943 Thomas Francis Woodlock, editor.
1944 Anne O'Hare McCormick, journalist.
1946 Dr. Carlton J. H. Hayes, historian, author and diplomat.

LITERARY PRIZES

Limited Editions Club Gold Medal

This medal is awarded periodically to "the American author of that book, published in the three years previous to the making of the award, which is considered most nearly to attain the stature of a classic."

1935 *An Almanac for Moderns,* by Donald Culross Peattie. (Putnam.)
1938 *The Flowering of New England,* by Van Wyck Brooks. (Dutton.)
1941 *For Whom the Bell Tolls,* by Ernest Hemingway. (Scribner.)
1945 *One Man's Meat,* by E. B. White. (Harper.)

The Loubat Prizes

The Loubat Prizes were instituted in 1893 by a grant of Joseph Florimond, Duc de Loubat. They consist of a first prize of $1,000 and a second prize of $400, offered every five years for the best work printed and published in the English language, on the history, geography, archaeology, ethnology, philology, or numismatics of North America. The fund is administered by Columbia University, New York, and the jury of awards is chosen from eminent men of learning. The competition for the prizes is open to all persons, whether connected with Columbia or not, and whether residents of the United States or not. Details of the award may be obtained from the Secretary of Columbia University, New York, N. Y. Previous winners may be found in the 1939 edition of *Famous Literary Prizes and Their Winners.*

1943 *The Inscriptions of Peten,* by Sylvanus Griswold Morley. (Carnegie Institution of Washington.)
    The Continental Congress, by Edmund Cody Burnett. (Macmillan.)

Mystery Novel Award

The Mystery Writers of America, Inc., 220 East 42nd Street, New York, N. Y., present an annual "Edgar Allan Poe" award for the best first mystery novel. The "Edgars" are copies of a special edition of *The Portable Poe* bound in red leather and are awarded in honor of the father of the detective story, Edgar Allan Poe.

1945 *Watchful at Night,* by Julius Fast. (Rinehart.)

AMERICAN PRIZES

New York University Literature Prize

The Gold Medal Award of the Society for the Libraries of New York University is offered for American authors "revealing new and distinctive talent in the field of imaginative literature." The first award was made in 1940. In March, 1943, it was announced that the award would be discontinued for the duration of the war. However, plans are being considered for resuming the award. It is expected that an award will be made in 1947. Further information may be obtained from the Society for the Libraries of New York University, New York University, Washington Square, New York.

1940 *Pale Horse, Pale Rider,* by Katherine Anne Porter. (Harcourt.)
1941 *Who Walk Alone,* by Perry Burgess. (Holt.)
1942 *The Trees,* by Conrad Richter. (Knopf.)

Ohioana Awards

In recent years there has been much interest in regional writers and groups in various states and sectors have offered prizes for regional material. However, among the most widely known and firmly established of these are the Ohioana Awards and the California Medals.

The Martha Kinney Cooper Ohioana Library was founded to honor Ohio writers, to acquaint the public with their books, to collect these books in one place and thereby preserve the culture and traditions of the state. In 1941 the Executive Board inaugurated a plan providing awards to a number of outstanding books. The prizes, which take the form of ceramic medals designed by Paul Bogataya, are awarded annually in the fall.

The Ohioana Library is the only one of its kind that has been developed wholly by private subscription and is unique in its wide promotion for Ohio authors. Further information concerning the awards may be obtained from Mrs. Depew Head, Ohioana Library, 1109 State Office Building, Columbus 15, Ohio.

1942 *Prelude to Victory,* by James B. Reston. (Knopf.)
1943 Fiction: *Bitter Honey,* by Martin Joseph Freeman. (Macmillan.)
  Non-fiction: *Climate Makes the Man,* by Clarence A. Mills. (Harper.)
  Juvenile: *Bibi: The Baker's Horse,* by Anna Bird Stewart. (Lippincott.)
1944 Fiction: *Take Nothing for Your Journey,* by Ann Steward. (Macmillan.)

Biography: *The Wright Brothers,* by Fred C. Kelly. (Harcourt.)
Juvenile: *Bayou Suzette,* by Lois Lenski. (Lippincott.)
Poetry: *Cloth of Tempest,* by Kenneth Patchen. (Harper.)
War Book: *Burma Surgeon,* by Gordon S. Seagrave. (Norton.)

1945 Fiction: *Deep River,* by Henrietta Buckmaster. (Harcourt.)
Non-fiction: *The Road to Teheran,* by Foster Rhea Dulles. (Princeton Univ. Press.)
Juvenile: *One God: The Ways We Worship Him,* by Florence Mary Fitch. (Lothrop, Lee & Shepard.)
Humor: *The Queen Was in the Kitchen,* by Daphne Alloway McVicker. (Whittlesey House.)
I Never Left Home, by Bob Hope. (Simon & Schuster.)

Pulitzer Prizes in Letters

The Pulitzer Prizes in Letters date from 1917. They were established by the terms of the will of Joseph Pulitzer (1847-1911) Mr. Pulitzer is remembered as the newspaper genius of the New York *World* and for his gift of a School of Journalism to Columbia University, as well as for his prizes to American literature.

Usually five prizes of $500 each (prior to 1942 these prizes were $1,000 each) are awarded in the field of letters. However, in 1941 and 1946 no award was given for a novel; in 1946 no poetry prize was given; in 1942 and 1944 no drama prize could be decided upon, although in the latter year a special award of $500 was given to Richard Rodgers and Oscar Hammerstein II for the operetta, *Oklahoma.* Since 1917 only two authors have refused the Pulitzer prizes: Sinclair Lewis in 1926 for *Arrowsmith* and William Saroyan in 1940 for his play, *The Time of Your Life.* A rather complete outline of the discussions centering around early Pulitzer prize winners will be found in the 1939 edition of *Famous Literary Prizes and Their Winners.*

In addition to prizes in letters, there are Pulitzer prizes in journalism, music, and traveling scholarships for graduates of the School of Journalism and students of the National Academy of Design. The terms of the awards, revised to May 1946, are as follows:

1. The award of prizes and traveling scholarships is made by the Trustees of Columbia University on the recommendation of the Advisory Board of the Graduate School of Journalism, and is usually announced during the month of May.

2. Nominations of candidates for any one of the Pulitzer Prizes

should be made in writing on or before February 1 of each year, addressed to the Secretary of Columbia University, New York, on forms which may be obtained on application to the Secretary of the University.

3. Each nomination must be accompanied by three copies of any book, or one copy of any editorial, article, or other material submitted by any competitor, or on his behalf. Books submitted in competition for the Prizes become the property of the University. In the case of a musical composition, performing organizations (orchestras, theaters, etc.) are requested to send nominations accompanied by one copy of the score. The Advisory Board, at its descretion, may waive the requirement of submission of the score of a musical work if warranted by special circumstances, for example, if there is only one existing score, indispensable for performance. Nomination of a play, opera, or ballet, should be made while it is being performed.

4. Competition for a prize will be limited, except in the case of the drama and music, to work done during the calendar year ending December 31 next preceding; consideration for the prizes in music and drama will be of works produced during the twelve months April 1 to March 31 inclusive.

5. The Advisory Board shall be under no obligation to pass upon the merits of any book, musical score, manuscript, editorial, article, or other literary material unless the same shall have been submitted in accordance with Paragraphs 2 and 3, preceding, but may do so at the request of any of its members.

6. If in any one year no book, play, or musical composition written for a prize offered shall be of sufficient excellence in the opinion of the Advisory Board, or if in any other subject of competition all the competitors shall fall below the standard of excellence fixed by the Advisory Board, then in that case the amount of such prize or prizes may be withheld in such year.

7. Nothing in this plan relating to the preliminary selection or nomination of candidates for the several prizes and traveling scholarships shall be deemed to limit in any way the authority and control of the Advisory Board, who may, at their discretion, modify any of the provisions relating to the preliminary selection or nomination of candidates.

8. Any author, composer, or journalist is eligible for consideration each year for any award, irrespective of the fact that he may have received a prize in any previous year.

LITERARY PRIZES

Prizes in Letters are made annually as follows:

1. For a distinguished novel published during the year by an American author, preferably dealing with American life, $500.

2. For the original American play, performed in New York, which shall represent in marked fashion the educational value and power of the stage, preferably dealing with American life, $500.

3. For a distinguished book of the year upon the history of the United States, $500.

4. For a distinguished American biography teaching patriotic and unselfish services to the people, illustrated by an eminent example, excluding, as too obvious, the names of George Washington and Abraham Lincoln, $500.

5. For a distinguished volume of verse published during the year by an American author, $500.

PULITZER PRIZE-WINNING NOVELS

1917 No award.
1918 *His Family,* by Ernest Poole. (Macmillan.)
1919 *The Magnificent Ambersons,* by Booth Tarkington. (Doubleday.)
1920 No award.
1921 *The Age of Innocence,* by Edith Wharton. (Appleton.)
1922 *Alice Adams,* by Booth Tarkington. (Doubleday.)
1923 *One of Ours,* by Willa Cather. (Knopf.)
1924 *The Able McLaughlins,* by Margaret Wilson. (Harper.)
1925 *So Big,* by Edna Ferber. (Doubleday.)
1926 *Arrowsmith,* by Sinclair Lewis. (Harcourt.)
1927 *Early Autumn,* by Louis Bromfield. (Stokes.)
1928 *The Bridge of San Luis Rey,* by Thornton Wilder. (Boni.)
1929 *Scarlet Sister Mary,* by Julia Peterkin. (Bobbs.)
1930 *Laughing Boy,* by Oliver La Farge. (Houghton.)
1931 *Years of Grace,* by Margaret Ayer Barnes. (Houghton.)
1932 *The Good Earth,* by Pearl S. Buck. (John Day.)
1933 *The Store,* by Thomas S. Stribling. (Doubleday.)
1934 *Lamb in His Bosom,* by Caroline Miller. (Harper.)
1935 *Now in November,* by Josephine W. Johnson. (Simon & Schuster.)
1936 *Honey in the Horn,* by Harold L. Davis. (Harper.)
1937 *Gone with the Wind,* by Margaret Mitchell. (Macmillan.)
1938 *The Late George Apley,* by John P. Marquand. (Little.)
1939 *The Yearling,* by Marjorie Kinnan Rawlings. (Scribner.)
1940 *The Grapes of Wrath,* by John Steinbeck. (Viking.)
1941 No award.
1942 *In This Our Life,* by Ellen Glasgow. (Harcourt.)
1943 *Dragon's Teeth,* by Upton Sinclair. (Viking.)
1944 *Journey in the Dark,* by Martin Flavin. (Harper.)
1945 *A Bell for Adano,* by John Hersey. (Knopf.)
1946 No award.

PULITZER PRIZE-WINNING DRAMAS

1917 No award.
1918 *Why Marry?* by Jesse Lynch Williams. (Scribner.)
1919 No award.
1920 *Beyond the Horizon,* by Eugene O'Neill. (Random.)
1921 *Miss Lulu Bett,* by Zona Gale. (Appleton.)
1922 *Anna Christie,* by Eugene O'Neill. (Random.)
1923 *Icebound,* by Owen Davis. (Little.)
1924 *Hell-Bent for Heaven,* by Hatcher Hughes. (Harper.)
1925 *They Knew What They Wanted,* by Sidney Howard. (Doubleday.)
1926 *Craig's Wife,* by George Kelly. (Little.)
1927 *In Abraham's Bosom,* by Paul Green. (McBride.)
1928 *Strange Interlude,* by Eugene O'Neill. (Random.)
1929 *Street Scene,* by Elmer Rice. (French.)
1930 *The Green Pastures,* by Marc Connelly. (Farrar & Rinehart.)
1931 *Alison's House,* by Susan Glaspell. (French.)
1932 *Of Thee I Sing,* by George S. Kaufman, Morrie Ryskind and Ira Gershwin. (Knopf.)
1933 *Both Your Houses,* by Maxwell Anderson. (French.)
1934 *Men in White,* by Sidney Kingsley. (Covici-Friede.)
1935 *The Old Maid,* by Zoë Akins. A dramatization of the novel by Edith Wharton. (Appleton.)
1936 *Idiot's Delight,* by Robert E. Sherwood. (Scribner.)
1937 *You Can't Take It With You,* by Moss Hart and George S. Kaufman. (Farrar & Rinehart.)
1938 *Our Town,* by Thornton Wilder. (Coward.)
1939 *Abe Lincoln in Illinois,* by Robert E. Sherwood. (Scribner.)
1940 *The Time of Your Life,* by William Saroyan. (Harcourt.)
1941 *There Shall Be No Night,* by Robert E. Sherwood. (Scribner.)
1942 No award.
1943 *The Skin of Our Teeth,* by Thorton Wilder. (Harper.)
1944 No drama award. Special award to *Oklahoma,* by Richard Rodgers and Oscar Hammerstein 2nd. (Random.)
1945 *Harvey,* by Mary Chase.
1946 *State of the Union,* by Howard Lindsay and Russel Crouse. (Random.)

PULITZER PRIZE-WINNING HISTORIES

1917 *With Americans of Past and Present Days,* by Jean Jules Jusserand. (Scribner.)
1918 *A History of the Civil War,* by James Ford Rhodes. (Macmillan.)
1919 No award.
1920 *The War with Mexico,* by Justin H. Smith. (Macmillan.)
1921 *The Victory at Sea,* by Rear Admiral William Snowden Sims, with the assistance of Burton J. Hendrick. (Doubleday.)
1922 *The Founding of New England,* by James Truslow Adams. (Little.)
1923 *The Supreme Court in United States History,* by Charles Warren. (Little.)

LITERARY PRIZES

1924 *The American Revolution: A Constitutional Interpretation,* by Charles Howard McIlwain. (Macmillan.)

1925 *A History of the American Frontier, 1763-1893,* by Frederic Logan Paxson. (Houghton.)

1926 *The History of the United States,* by Edward Channing. (Macmillan.)

1927 *Pinckney's Treaty: A Study of America's Advantage from Europe's Distress,* by Samuel Flagg Bemis. (John Hopkins Press.)

1928 *Main Currents in American Thought,* by Vernon Louis Parrington. (Harcourt.)

1929 *Organization and Administration of the Union Army 1861-1865,* by Fred Albert Shannon. (A. H. Clark.)

1930 *The War of Independence,* by Claude H. Van Tyne. (Houghton.)

1931 *The Coming of the War: 1914,* by Bernadotte Everly Schmitt. (Scribner.)

1932 *My Experiences in the World War,* by General John J. Pershing. (Stokes.)

1933 *The Significance of Sections in American History,* by Frederick Jackson Turner. (Holt.)

1934 *The People's Choice,* by Herbert Agar. (Houghton.)

1935 *The Colonial Period of American History,* by Charles McLean Andrews. (Yale.)

1936 *The Constitutional History of the United States,* by Andrew Cunningham McLaughlin. (Appleton.)

1937 *The Flowering of New England,* by Van Wyck Brooks. (Dutton.)

1938 *The Road to Reunion, 1865-1900,* by Paul Herman Buck. (Little.)

1939 *A History of American Magazines,* by Frank Luther Mott. (Harvard.)

1940 *Abraham Lincoln: The War Years,* by Carl Sandburg. (Harcourt.)

1941 *The Atlantic Migration, 1607-1860,* by Marcus Lee Hansen. (Harvard.)

1942 *Reveille in Washington,* by Margaret Leech. (Harper.)

1943 *Paul Revere and the World He Lived In,* by Esther Forbes. (Houghton.)

1944 *The Growth of American Thought,* by Merle Curti. (Harper.)

1945 *Unfinished Business,* by Stephen Bonsal. (Doubleday.)

1946 *The Age of Jackson,* by Arthur Schlesinger, Jr. (Little.)

PULITZER PRIZE-WINNING BIOGRAPHIES

1917 *Julia Ward Howe, 1819-1910,* by Laura E. Richards and Maud Howe Elliott, assisted by Florence Howe Hall. (Houghton.)

1918 *Benjamin Franklin, Self-Revealed,* by William Cabell Bruce. (Putnam.)

1919 *The Education of Henry Adams,* by Henry Adams. (Houghton.)

1920 *The Life of John Marshall,* by Albert J. Beveridge. (Houghton.)

1921 *The Americanization of Edward Bok,* by Edward Bok. (Scribner.)

1922 *A Daughter of the Middle Border,* by Hamlin Garland. (Macmillan.)

1923 *Life and Letters of Walter Hines Page,* edited by Burton J. Hendrick. (Houghton; abridged ed., Doubleday.)

AMERICAN PRIZES

1924 *From Immigrant to Inventor*, by Michael Idvorsky Pupin. (Scribner.)

1925 *Barrett Wendell and His Letters*, by M. A. DeWolfe Howe. (Little.)

1926 *Life of Sir William Osler*, by Harvey Cushing. (Oxford.)

1927 *Whitman, an Interpretation in Narrative*, by Emory Holloway. (Knopf.)

1928 *The American Orchestra and Theodore Thomas*, by Charles Edward Russell. (Doubleday.)

1929 *The Training of an American: The Earlier Life and Letters of Walter Hines Page*, by Burton J. Hendrick. (Houghton.)

1930 *The Raven: A Biography of Sam Houston*, by Marquis James. (Bobbs.)

1931 *Charles W. Eliot*, by Henry James. (Houghton.)

1932 *Theodore Roosevelt*, by Henry Pringle. (Harcourt.)

1933 *Grover Cleveland*, by Allan Nevins. (Dodd.)

1934 *John Hay: From Poetry to Politics*, by Tyler Dennett. (Dodd.)

1935 *R. E. Lee: A Biography*, by Douglas Southall Freeman. (Sribner.)

1936 *The Thought and Character of William James*, by Ralph Barton Perry. (Little.)

1937 *Hamilton Fish: The Inner History of the Grant Administration*, by Allan Nevins. (Dodd.)

1938 *Pedlar's Progress; The Life of Bronson Alcott,* by Odell Shepard. (Little.)
Andrew Jackson, by Marquis James. (Bobbs.)

1939 *Benjamin Franklin*, by Carl Van Doren. (Viking.)

1940 *Woodrow Wilson. Life and Letters*, Vol. VII and VIII, by Ray Stannard Baker. (Doubleday.)

1941 *Jonathan Edwards*, by Ola Elizabeth Winslow. (Macmillan.)

1942 *Crusader in Crinoline*, by Forrest Wilson. (Lippincott.)

1943 *Admiral of the Ocean Sea*, by Samuel Eliot Morison. (Little.)

1944 *The American Leonardo: The Life of Samuel F. B. Morse,* by Carleton Mabee. (Knopf.)

1945 *George Bancroft: Brahmin Rebel,* by Russel Blaine Nye. (Knopf.)

1946 *Son of the Wilderness*, by Linnie Marsh Wolfe. (Knopf.)

PULITZER PRIZE-WINNING POETRY

The Pulitzer Prizes in Letters were only four in number until 1922, when a fifth prize was added for Poetry. Before this prize was established, awards in poetry were made from gifts provided by the Poetry Society to Sara Teasdale in 1918; to Margaret Widdemer and Carl Sandburg in 1919.

1922 *Collected Poems*, by Edwin Arlington Robinson. (Macmillan.)

1923 *The Ballad of the Harp-Weaver; A Few Figs from Thistles*, by Edna St. Vincent Millay. (Harper.)

1924 *New Hampshire*, by Robert Frost. (Holt.)

1925 *The Man Who Died Twice,* by Edwin Arlington Robinson. (Macmillan.)
1926 *What's O'Clock,* by Amy Lowell. (Houghton.)
1927 *Fiddler's Farewell,* by Leonora Speyer. (Knopf.)
1928 *Tristram,* by Edwin Arlington Robinson. (Macmillan.)
1929 *John Brown's Body,* by Stephen Vincent Benét. (Farrar & Rinehart.)
1930 *Selected Poems,* by Conrad Aiken. (Scribner.)
1931 *Collected Poems,* by Robert Frost. (Holt.)
1932 *The Flowering Stone,* by George Dillon. (Viking.)
1933 *Conquistador,* by Archibald MacLeish. (Houghton.)
1934 *Collected Verse,* by Robert Hillyer. (Knopf.)
1935 *Bright Ambush,* by Audrey Wurdemann. (John Day.)
1936 *Strange Holiness,* by Robert P. T. Coffin. (Macmillan.)
1937 *A Further Range,* by Robert Frost. (Holt.)
1938 *Cold Morning Sky,* by Marya Zaturenska. (Macmillan.)
1939 *Selected Poems,* by John Gould Fletcher. (Farrar & Rinehart.)
1940 *Collected Poems,* by Mark Van Doren. (Holt.)
1941 *Sunderland Capture,* by Leonard Bacon. (Harper.)
1942 *The Dust Which Is God,* by William Rose Benét. (Dodd.)
1943 *A Witness Tree,* by Robert Frost. (Holt.)
1944 *Western Star,* by Stephen Vincent Benét. (Farrar & Rinehart.)
1945 *V-Letter and Other Poems,* by Karl Shapiro. (Reynal.)
1946 No award.

An Anthology of Pulitzer Prize Poems 1922-1941, (Random.) contains important selections from every book of poetry that won the Pulitzer Prize to 1941.

Roosevelt Medal

The Roosevelt Awards, established by the Roosevelt Memorial Association in 1923, are given annually in certain fields associated with Theodore Roosevelt's career: public and international law, industrial peace, science, historical literature, conservation of natural resources, leadership of youth, etc.

Following is a list of recipients in the literary field who have received the award since 1938. Previous winners in this field can be found in the 1939 edition of *Famous Literary Prizes and Their Winners.*

1939 Carl Sandburg, poet.
1942 Booth Tarkington, novelist.

Constance Lindsay Skinner Award

This award, a bronze plaque given by the Women's National Book Association, was established in 1940 in honor of the late

Constance Lindsay Skinner, distinguished author and editor. The medal is presented each year to a woman in the book world, in recognition of outstanding work in her field. Although this is not specifically a *literary* prize, it is a book trade award and has been awarded to authors.

1940 Anne Carroll Moore, librarian.
1941 Blair Niles, author.
1942 Irita Van Doren, editor.
1943 Mary Graham Bonner, author.
1944 Mildred C. Smith, editor.
1945 Lillian Smith, author.
1946 Amy Loveman, editor.

Southern Authors' Award

The Southern Women's National Democratic Organization in New York, Inc. offers an annual award of $150 for the most distinguished book by a Southern author on some phase of Southern life. The organization sponsors an annual luncheon, held in January at a New York hotel, at which time the award is made.

In 1940 *The Web and the Rock* received "premier recognition of merit" but, as the purpose of the award is to encourage living writers, the prize went to Mr. Basso whose book was rated by the judges as second in merit.

Details concerning the award may be obtained from Mrs. Winifred Kittredge, 88 Morningside Drive, New York, N. Y.

1938 *The Old South; Struggles for Democracy*, by William E. Dodd. (Macmillan.)
1939 *Blow for a Landing*, by Ben Lucien Burman. (John Day.)
1940 *Days Before Lent*, by Hamilton Basso. (Scribner.)
     The Web and the Rock, by Thomas Wolfe. (Harper.)
1941 *The River of Earth*, by James Still. (Viking.)
1942 *In This Our Life*, by Ellen Glasgow. (Harcourt.)
1943 *Lee's Lieutenants*, by Douglas Southall Freeman. (Scribner.)
1944 *Judah P. Benjamin, Confederate Statesman*, by Robert Douthat Meade. (Oxford.)
1945 *The Winds of Fear*, by Hodding Carter. (Farrar & Rinehart.)
1946 *Three O'Clock Dinner*, by Josephine Pinckney. (Viking.)

The Spingarn Medal

This gold medal, presented annually to an American Negro for the highest and noblest achievement of the year was instituted by Joel E. Spingarn in 1914 and is awarded by the National

Association for the Advancement of Colored People, 20 West 40th Street, New York 18, N. Y. After Mr. Spingarn's death in 1939 the award was continued from a fund set up by his will. The medal has been awarded to outstanding Negroes in the fields of music, education, science, medicine, politics, literature, etc. The list of winners below includes only those who received the award for achievement in literature.

1918 William S. Braithwaite, poet, critic, editor.
1920 William E. B. DuBois, editor of "The Crisis."
1925 James Weldon Johnson, poet.
1926 Carter Godwin Woodson, author and editor.
1928 Charles W. Chestnutt, novelist.
1941 Richard Wright, author.

James Terry White Medal

The James Terry White Medal was first offered in 1938, to be awarded to a member of the American Library Association for "notable published professional writing." The award was made annually at the convention of the American Library Association, but was discontinued in 1941.

1938 *Government of the American Public Library,* by Carleton B. Joeckel. (Univ. of Chicago Press.)
1939 *The Geography of Reading,* by Louis R. Wilson. (Univ. of Chicago Press and A. L. A.)
1940 No award.
1941 *Reading With Children,* by Anne T. Eaton. (Viking.)

Writers' Conferences

Every year at the various summer writers' conferences, prizes are offered for manuscripts submitted by the attending students. The prizes are too numerous and too varied from year to year to be listed in a book of this scope. However, the importance of these conferences should not be overlooked. In the past few years the important conferences have been: Bread Loaf Writers' Conference, Middlebury, Vermont; University of New Hampshire Writers' Conference, Durham, New Hampshire; Midwestern Writers' Conference, Northwestern University, Evanston, Illinois; Indiana University Writers' Conference; University of Wisconsin Writers' Conference; Olivet Writers' Conference, Michigan; University of Colorado Writers' Conference, Boulder, Colorado; Writers' Conference of the West, Oakland, California; Pacific Northwest Writers' Conference, University of Washington.

The seriousness and breadth of the work involved may be judged by the recognized merit of the teachers and lecturers employed at the conferences. The following is but a brief list of important figures in American literature who have participated: Robert Frost, Louis Untermeyer, James T. Farrell, Robert E. Sherwood, Paul Green, Robert P. Tristram Coffin, Louis Adamic, Carl Sandburg, Katherine Anne Porter, Sherwood Anderson.

The prizes offered each year range in value from $25 prizes for a sonnet to the $250 novel awards offered by the Thomas Y. Crowell Company and Farrar and Rinehart at the Midwestern Writers' Conference. The following publications and organizations have, in the past few years, sponsored awards of varying amounts at the Writers' Conferences: *American Weave;* Chicago *Daily News;* Chicago *Sun; Coronet* Magazine; Thomas Y. Crowell Company; Dodd, Mead and Company; Doubleday - Curtis Brown; Farrar and Rinehart; National Broadcasting Company; Quarrie Corporation; *Rewrite;* A. A. Wyn.

PUBLISHERS' PRIZES

Abingdon-Cokesbury Award

In 1944 the Abingdon-Cokesbury Press offered a prize of $500 for the best book by a new writer. There was no stipulation as to the character of the text except that it should be over 40,000 words and that the writer should have in mind the fact that Abingdon-Cokesbury publishes religious books.

1944 *The Crisis of Faith,* by Dr. Stanley R. Hopper.

All-Nations Prize Novel Contest

In 1936 and in 1939 this international prize novel competition was conducted by Farrar and Rinehart in cooperation with the Literary Guild and eleven publishers in as many countries. The prize in the first contest was $20,000; in the second, $15,000. In both cases the American entry received a prize of $1,000.

1936 *Street of the Fishing Cat,* by Jolán Foldes, Hungarian.
       Steps Going Down, by John T. McIntyre. American entry.
1939 *No Arms, No Armour,* by Robert D. Q. Henriques, English.
       Sam, by John Selby. American entry.

Atlantic Monthly Prizes

NOVEL PRIZE

This prize, inaugurated in 1927 by the *Atlantic Monthly* and Little, Brown & Company, offers a prize of $10,000. The object of the award is "to secure a distinctive and interesting novel and make it one of the outstanding books of the year." No contest has been held since 1942, at which time no award was made.

The 1947 competition, which closes January 15, 1947, will admit, for the first time in the history of this award, manuscripts written in foreign languages as well as in English. There are no restrictions as to author or subject. Details concerning the award may be obtained from the *Atlantic Monthly* Press, 8 Arlington Street, Boston 8, Mass.

1927 *Jalna,* by Mazo de la Roche.
1930 Contest held, but no prize awarded.
1932 *Peking Picnic,* by Ann Bridge.
1934 *Dusk at the Grove,* by Samuel Rogers.
1936 *I Am the Fox,* by Winifred Mayne Van Etten.
1938 Contest held, but no prize awarded.
1940 *The Family,* by Nina Fedorova.
1942 Contest held, no awards made.

LITERARY PRIZES

"ATLANTIC FIRST" STORY AWARD

In 1946 the *Atlantic Monthly* announced an annual award for *"Atlantic* Firsts", stories by new writers, in a competition designed to encourage new writers. The editors of the *Atlantic* have reserved space in each issue for *"Atlantic* Firsts". The most promising story published in each six-month period (January - June; July - December) will be awarded $1500 by the *Atlantic,* in cooperation with Metro-Goldwyn-Mayer. A second prize of $750 will be given. The stories submitted should be from 2,000 to 20,000 words in length; neither one-act plays nor scenarios are eligible. If any of the winners have film possibilities, Metro-Goldwyn-Mayer will have option to buy any of them at $5,000 each.

January - June 1946   *Waves of Darkness,* by Cord Meyer, Jr. First prize.
                      Night Watch, by Thomas Heggen. Second Prize.
                      (Published by Houghton as *Mister Roberts.*)

ATLANTIC MONTHLY — LITTLE, BROWN
NON-FICTION CONTEST

Beginning in 1929 this contest was held every two years with a prize of $5,000. In 1943 a Victory Contest replaced this award, but no prize was given. After 1943 the contest was discontinued.

1929   *Grandmother Brown's Hundred Years,* by Harriet Connor Brown.
1931   *Forty-Niners,* by Archer Butler Hulbert.
1933   *Poor Splendid Wings; The Rossettis and Their Circle,* by Frances Winwar.
1935   *Old Jules,* by Mari Sandoz.
1937   Contest omitted because of Little, Brown Centenary Contest.
1939   *The Land Below the Wind,* by Agnes Keith.
1941   *Tomorrow Will Come,* by E. M. Almedingen.
1943   No award.

A. S. Barnes Servicemen's Poetry Contest

In 1943 A. S. Barnes and Company sponsored a poetry contest for members of the armed forces. The awards ranged from $250 to $5. The one hundred and twenty-five winning poems were published in book form under the title *Reveille.*

1943   John Ackerson — first prize.
       Harold Applebaum — second prize.
       Charles E. Butler — third prize.
       Arthur Gordon — fourth prize.
       Neal A. Harper — fifth prize.

Bruce Publishing Company Prizes

BRUCE — *EXTENSION* NOVEL PRIZE

In 1943 the Bruce Publishing Company of Milwaukee, in cooperation with *Extension Magazine* of Chicago sponsored a $500 prize novel competition. The contest was open to citizens of the United States and residents of Canada who were over twenty years of age for a novel "of high literary quality, and handled in the light of Catholic understanding and teaching."

1944 *The Scarlet Lily,* by Edward F. Murphy.

BRUCE FELLOWSHIPS

The Bruce Publishing Company has established four annual author fellowships, one in biography and three in fiction. These fellowships are open to any Catholic lay person and are offered "in an effort to meet more adequately the need for good novels and biographies among a growing number of Catholic readers, and to encourage potential lay Catholic authors to write." Each fellowship pays the holder $1,200, payable in twelve monthly installments. Complete rules of the offer may be obtained from The Bruce Publishing Company, 540 North Michigan Street, Milwaukee 1, Wisconsin.

1946 *The Flight of the Swan,* by Margaret Ann Hubbard. Fiction.

Carey-Thomas Award

The Carey-Thomas Award was established in 1942 by *The Publishers' Weekly,* the American book trade journal, as a means of honoring publishing firms for carefully planned enterprises — not credit for editorial judgment alone, or production and promotion alone, but for all the elements that make for good publishing: the creative idea, cooperation with the author, careful production and imagination, and successful marketing. "The conception of just what constitutes good publishing can be studied only from examples," state the donors, "and if over the years competent judges point out where excellence lies, the accumulating record will help visualize what good publishing is and will encourage more enterprises of equal standard."

A jury composed of two critics, a bookseller, an author and a librarian is appointed annually by *The Publishers' Weekly* and its decision is announced in January to cover publication of the preceding year. The award, which takes the form of a printed certificate, bears the names of two early American publishers who had the special qualities which must be brought together if the best of publishing is to be achieved—Mathew Carey of Philadelphia and Isaiah Thomas of Worcester.

1943 Farrar & Rinehart for *The Rivers of America* Series.

1944 University of Chicago Press for *A Dictionary of American English on Historical Principles.*

1945 E. P. Dutton & Company for *The World of Washington Irving,* by Van Wyck Brooks.

1946 Alfred A. Knopf, Inc. for *The American Language,* by H. L. Mencken.

Thomas Y. Crowell Fiction Fellowships

The Thomas Y. Crowell Company, in cooperation with the *University of Kansas City Review,* the *Prairie Schooner,* and the School of Letters of University of Iowa, sponsored a series of six Fiction Fellowships of $500 each. The competition, judged on the basis of four chapters and outline of a proposed novel, was open to authors whose work had appeared in either of the magazines and to past, present and future members of the School of Letters.

1946 *The Color of Blood,* by Ralph Rundell.
Cut Down Out of Time, by Ruth Schellin.

Dial Press Awards

TEACHERS' AWARD

In 1939 the Dial Press offered a prize of $1,000 for the best original novel with a scholastic background in which the protagonist is a public school teacher. The contest was open only to persons teaching in the public school system.

1940 *Miss Munday,* by Sophia Engstrand.

NOVEL CONTEST

The Dial Press Novel Contest of 1942 was open to writers under thirty-five years of age who had not had a novel published. The prize of $1,000 was offered for "an outstanding novel of high literary quality that concerned itself realistically with the problems of adjustment facing the young men and women of America today."

1942 *The Gates of Aulis,* by Gladys Schmitt.

AMERICAN PRIZES

NOVELETTE CONTEST

In 1944 the Dial Press, in cooperation with the *Partisan Review,* sponsored a novelette contest. The winning entries were published in the *Partisan Review.* The first prize was $500, the second $250. Two third prizes of $100 each were given.

1945 *The Colony,* by Isaac Rosenfeld. First prize.
      The Home Front, by Jean Stafford. Second prize.
      The Red-Headed Girl, by Barbara Gibbs. Third prize.
      The Scoutmaster, by Peter Taylor. Third prize.

Dodd, Mead and Company Awards

NON-FICTION FELLOWSHIPS

An award of $1,500 was offered by Dodd, Mead to graduate students in American and Canadian colleges and universities for an outstanding piece of non-fiction. A $2,000 prize was offered to members of the regular teaching staff, research associates or professors emeriti in American and Canadian universities. This award was also open to college teachers on sabbatical leave or leave for special research. The contest closed October 1, 1946. Complete details may be obtained from Dodd, Mead and Company, 432 Fourth Ave., New York 16, N. Y.

DODD, MEAD - *REDBOOK* NOVEL AWARD

Dodd, Mead Publishing Company, in conjunction with *Redbook* magazine offers $10,000 for a winning novel. The competition is open to any American or Canadian author who has not published more than two novels in book form or serially. The 1946 competition closed August 1, 1946. Information can be obtained from *Redbook* Magazine, 230 Park Avenue, New York 17, N. Y.

1925 *Wild Geese,* by Martha Ostenso. (In cooperation with *Pictorial Review* & Famous Players-Lasky Corp.)
1927 *Rebellion,* by Mateel Howe Farnham. (In cooperation with *Pictorial Review* & First National Pictures.)
1933 *Candy,* by L. M. Alexander. (In cooperation with *Pictorial Review.*)
1935 *The Old Ashburn Place,* by Margaret Flint. (In cooperation with *Pictorial Review.*)
1937 *Young Doctor Galahad,* by Elizabeth Seifert. (In cooperation with *Redbook.*)
1940 *Hildreth,* by Harlow Estes.
1942 *Turning Leaves,* by Ellen Proctor.
1944 *They Dare Not Go A'Hunting,* by Dorothea Cornwell.

LITERARY PRIZES

RED BADGE CONTEST

A prize of $1,000 plus royalties is offered for the best mystery detective novel by an American or Canadian author. In 1941 the contest, which had been held annually, was changed to a semi-annual competition.

1936   *The Affair of the Scarlet Crab,* by Clifford Knight.
1937   *Fast Company,* by Marco Page.
1938   *Cancelled in Red,* by Hugh Pentecost.
1939   *A Matter of Iodine,* by David Keith.
1941   Spring. *Lady in Lilac,* by Susannah Shane..
       Fall.   *Murder A La Mode,* by Eleanore Kelly Sellars.
1942   Spring. *Heads You Lose,* by Christianna Brand.
       Fall.   *The Snake in the Grass,* by James Howard Wellard.
1943   Spring. *Too Many Bones,* by Ruth Sawtell Wallis.
       Fall.   No award.
1944   Spring. *The Man with the Lumpy Nose,* by Lawrence Larier.
       Fall.   No award.
1945   Spring. *Appointment in Manila,* by Elinor Chamberlain.
       Fall.   *Hangman's Hill,* by Franklyn Pell.
1946   Spring. *This Deadly Dark,* by Lee Wilson.

INTERCOLLEGIATE LITERARY FELLOWSHIP

The Dodd, Mead Intercollegiate Fellowship has been established for men and women students in American colleges and universities who wish to become professional authors. The amount of the fellowship is $1,200, given annually. It includes students in both the United States and Canada. Terms of the award may be obtained from Dodd. Mead and Company, 432 Fourth Avenue, New York 16, N. Y.

1941   *Seventeenth Summer,* by Maureen Daly, Rosary College, Illinois.
1942   *Hedge Against the Sun,* by Barbara Bentley, Pomona College, California.
1943   *The Narrowing Wind,* by Catherine Lawrence, Wellesley College, Massachusetts.
1944   *The Heart and the Shuttle,* by Mary Vardoulakis, Wellesley College, Massachusetts.
1945   *City in the Sun,* by Karon Kehoe, Hunter College, New York.
       The Unreasoning Heart, by Constance Beresford-Howe, McGill University, Montreal.
1946   *Field of Old Blood,* by Hilda Osterhout, Vassar College, New York.

AMERICAN PRIZES

Doubleday and Company Prizes

DOUBLEDAY PRIZE NOVEL AWARD

An award of $20,000, of which $10,000 is a cash award and $10,000 an advance against royalties, was announced in 1944 by Doubleday and Company. The competition, not limited to first novels is open to new or established writers of any nationality. There are no restrictions as to theme, but the book must be written in English. The award is given to the novel which best combines literary distinction and popular appeal. The publishers reserve the right to withhold the award if no manuscript of sufficient merit is received.

1945   *Before the Sun Goes Down*, by Elizabeth Metzger Howard.
1946   *Black Fountains*, by Oswald Wynd.

THE GEORGE WASHINGTON CARVER MEMORIAL AWARD

The George Washington Carver Award, first announced in December of 1943, is offered by Doubleday and Company for "any work of fiction, non-fiction or poetry which seems to the judges (the editors of Doubleday and Company) to make an effective contribution to the Negro's place in American life." The prize is $2,500 ($1,500 outright and $1,000 as an advance against royalties) and will remain open indefinitely at the discretion of the publishers.

1945   *Mrs. Palmer's Honey*, by Fannie Cook.

DOUBLEDAY-*KENYON REVIEW* SHORT STORY CONTEST

The short story competition sponsored by Doubleday and Company in cooperation with the *Kenyon Review* offers a first prize of $500 and a second prize of $250 for a short story by an author who has never published a book of fiction. Inquiries concerning the competition should be addressed to the *Kenyon Review*, Gambier, Ohio.

In 1946 the prize money was divided equally into two first prizes of $375 each.

1944   *The Snowfall*, by Jean Garrique. First Prize.
         A Piece of Bread, by Frances Gray Patton. Second Prize.
1945   *The Imaginary Jew*, by John Berryman. First Prize.
         The Bell, by Mona Van Duym. Second Prize.
1946   *You Can Wreck It*, by Walter Elder.
         You Never Go Back to Sleep, by Arthur Mizener.

LITERARY PRIZES

DOUBLEDAY — TWENTIETH CENTURY-FOX
NEW WRITERS CONTEST

This competition, which ran from October 1, 1944 to February 1, 1945, was designed to encourage those who had neither the time nor the money to complete novels on which they had begun work. The total prize amounted to $4,000.

1945 *But We Had Fun,* by Charles Andrews Fenton.

E. P. Dutton and Company Prizes

THE THOMAS JEFFERSON SOUTHERN AWARD

An annual literary award of $2,500, known as the Thomas Jefferson Southern Award, is offered by E. P. Dutton and Company for the best book manuscript submitted by a Southern author. The winner receives with the award, $1,500 of which is an advance against royalties, the Thomas Jefferson Gold Medal. The contest is open to authors born in the South, regardless of present residence, and to those who have lived in the South for at least five years, regardless of place of birth. The offer is open to new and established writers and includes fiction and non-fiction. The setting and subject-matter need not be Southern. Inquiries concerning the contest should be sent to The Thomas Jefferson Southern Award Contest, E. P. Dutton and Company, Inc., 300 Fourth Avenue, New York 10.

1942 *Mr. George's Joint,* by Elizabeth Lee Wheaton.
Special Silver Medal given to Eloise Liddon for *Some Lose Their Way.*
1943 No award given.
1944 *Taps for Private Tussie,* by Jesse Stuart.
1945 *Rooster Crows for Day,* by Ben Lucien Burman.

THE LEWIS AND CLARK NORTHWEST CONTEST

E. P. Dutton and Company offers annually a cash award of $2,500 against royalties for the best book manuscript submitted by an author from Washington, Oregon, Idaho, Montana or Alaska. $1,250 of the award will be paid on acceptance, and $1,250 on publication. The competition is open to all persons born in this area regardless of present residence, to persons who have lived there for at least five years, regardless of place of birth, and to any present student or graduate of a recognized college or university in the Northwest. It is also open to anyone who has completed a recognized course in English Literature or Creative Writing in this region, regardless of place of birth or residence. In 1946 the prize was increased to $3,000.

No award has been made in this competition since 1943.

1943 *The Glittering Hill,* by Clyde F. Murphy.

DUTTON SPORTS STORY AWARD

A prize of $500 is offered by E. P. Dutton & Co. for the best sports story of the year and a $100 award is offered for the best sports photograph. Sports editors of newspapers and magazines are invited to compete in the contest which covers feature articles, human interest items, and straight sports coverage stories. This contest is an annual event and an anthology, *The Fifty Best Sports Stories of 19—,* is published each year. Details may be secured from E. P. Dutton & Co., 300 Fourth Ave., New York 10, N. Y.

1944 Story: Al Laney, *New York Herald Tribune.*
1945 Story award split three ways.
      Jerry Nason, *Boston Globe.*
      Jimmy Powers, *New York Daily News.*
      Carol Hughes, *Coronet.*
      Photograph: Carmen Reporto, *Chicago Sun.*

Mary Roberts Rinehart Mystery Prize Contest

In 1939, in celebration of the thirtieth anniversary of Mary Roberts Rinehart's first mystery story, Farrar and Rinehart offered an award of $1,000 for the best mystery novel submitted. It was open to writers who had never before had a mystery story published in book form. In 1942 the contest was conducted in cooperation with *Collier's Weekly* and offered a prize of $2,000. The competition has been discontinued.

1940 *I Wanted to Murder,* by Clarissa Fairchild Cushman.
1941 *Justice be Damned,* by A. R. Hilliard.
1942 *The Rat Began to Gnaw the Rope,* by C. W. Grafton.

Frederick Fell Prize Novel Contest

The Frederick Fell Prize Novel Contest offers $3,000 as an immediate advance against royalties and guarantees a minimum $10,000 advertising campaign. The competition places no restrictions on setting or theme and is not limited to first novels. Details may be obtained from Frederick Fell, Inc., 386 Fourth Ave., New York 16, N. Y.

1944 *Winds, Blow Gently,* by Ronald Kirkbride.
1945 No award.

Harper and Brothers Prizes

HARPER PRIZE NOVEL CONTEST

The Harper Prize Novel Competitions have been conducted in the uneven numbered years since 1923. The competition is designed to give recognition to a work of outstanding merit in the field of fiction. In 1939 a prize of $7,500 was offered for the best novel submitted by an American author who had not published a novel before January 1, 1924. In 1941 the amount of the award was increased to $10,000. Of this, $2,000 is an outright prize. In 1945 the rules of the contest were amended so as not to exclude authors of previously published work.

1923 *The Able McLaughlins,* by Margaret Wilson.
1925 *The Perennial Bachelor,* by Anne Parrish.
1927 *The Grandmothers,* by Glenway Westcott.
1929 *The Dark Journey,* by Julian Green.
1931 *Brother in the West,* by Robert Raynolds.
1933 *The Fault of Angels,* by Paul Horgan.
1935 *Honey in the Horn,* by H. L. Davis.
1937 *The Seven Who Fled,* by Frederic Prokosch.
1939 *Children of God,* by Vardis Fisher
1941 *Marriage Is a Private Affair,* by Judith Kelly.
1943 *Journey in the Dark,* by Martin Flavin.
1945 *Wasteland,* by Jo Sinclair.

HARPER'S 125th ANNIVERSARY NON-FICTION AWARD

In 1942 Harper and Brothers offered a prize of $12,500 to any author, new or unknown, regardless of age or nationality, for a work of non-fiction. The contest was part of the celebration of the 125th anniversary of the founding of Harper and Brothers. The award was divided between two books.

1943 *Memories of Happy Days,* by Julian Green
      I Came Out of the Eighteenth Century, by John Andrew Rice.

EUGENE SAXTON MEMORIAL FELLOWSHIPS

The Eugene F. Saxton Memorial Trust has been established by Harper and Brothers in memory of the late Eugene F. Saxton, for many years head editor of Harper. The purpose of the

memorial trust, which was founded in 1944, is to offer fellowships with substantial grants of money to creative writers, especially new ones who lack publishing connections and financial
means. Authors who receive these fellowships will be free to
arrange for publication of their books with any publishing house
they may choose. The fellowships have no fixed value, and may
be contributed to from time to time. The entire administration
of the funds and other matters concerning the fellowship are in
the hands of a board of three trustees: Martha P. Saxton, widow
of Eugene F. Saxton; Amy Loveman, associate editor of the
Saturday Review of Literature and head of the editorial department of the Book-of-the-Month Club; and Edward C. Aswell,
editor of general publications for Harper.

The general rule, except for unusual circumstances, is that the
fellowship in each case will not exceed $2,500 in any one year,
and this amount will be an outright grant and in no part return-
able. All applications will be considered as soon as possible and
may be filed at any time. These may be secured from the Eugene
F. Saxton Memorial Trust, Harper and Brothers, 49 East 33rd
Street, New York 16, N. Y.

1945 Richard Plant.
1946 James A. Baldwin; Celia Chao; Charles H. Miller.

Houghton Mifflin Prizes
LIFE IN AMERICA AWARDS

Houghton Mifflin offers a prize of $2,500 for manuscripts to
be published in a series of books called *Life in America.* "A prize-
winning manuscript may be the life story of a man or woman of
any profession, business or occupation. It may be written in the
first person by the subject of the book, it may be the biography
of someone of this or an earlier generation, or it may deal with
some important aspect of America as expressed in the lives of its
people. The only qualification is that it shall definitely contribute
to the understanding of our country by presenting a true and
vivid account of life in America."

Writers intending to submit manuscripts may send in an application blank signifying their intention. Further details may be
obtained from the *Life in America* Editor, Houghton Mifflin
Company, 2 Park Street, Boston 7, Massachusetts.

1941 *No Life for a Lady,* by Agnes Morley Cleaveland.
      The Road of a Naturalist, by Donald Culross Peattie.

LITERARY PRIZES

1942   *Small Town South,* by Sam Byrd.
      Safe Deliverance, by Dr. Frederick C. Irving.
1943   *New World A-Coming,* by Roi Ottley.
      When Johnny Comes Marching Home, by Dixon Wecter.
1944   No awards made.
1945   *No Time for Tears,* by Lora Wood Hughes.
1946   *First Flowers of Our Wilderness,* by James Thomas Flexner.
      The Wallaces of Iowa, by Russell Lord.

HOUGHTON MIFFLIN LITERARY FELLOWSHIPS

In the hope of encouraging writers of promise and of helping them to secure the financial independence essential to their development, the Houghton Mifflin Company offers two literary fellowships. These Fellowships, which may be given for any type of literature, are intended for men and women of creative ability and of high intellectual and personal qualifications. The Fellowships were originally $1,000; were later increased to $1,500 and, in 1944, to $2,400, in addition to subsequent royalties. In special cases a Fellowship may be extended for a second year.

The candidates must submit samples of past work, published or unpublished, as well as definite plans for their projects and the names of three responsible persons who can vouch for their character and qualifications.

In 1944, in commemoration of the tenth anniversary of the Fellowship Awards, a special Poetry Prize Fellowship of $1,000 was offered.

1935   *Green Margins,* by E. P. O'Donnell.
      Spanish Prelude, by Jenny Ballou.
1936   *Night Rider,* by Robert Penn Warren.
      Point Noir, Clelie Huggins.
1937   *Old Haven,* by David Cornel DeJong.
      Young Man With a Horn, by Dorothy Baker.
1938   *The Giant Joshua,* by Maurine Whipple.
      Second fellowship not awarded.
1939   *Quincie Bolliver,* by Mary King.
      A Man Named Grant, by Helen Todd.
1940   *Cone of Silence,* by A. Fleming McLiesh.
      Old Bullion, by Mary Benton.
1941   No Fellowships awarded.
1942   *Dwight Craig: A Success Story,* by Donald MacRae.
1943   No Fellowships awarded.
1944   *Day of Vision,* by Edward Kimbrough.
      Looking for a Bluebird, by Joseph Wechsberg.
      Special Poetry Award to *North and South,* by Elizabeth Bishop.

1945 *The Street,* by Ann Petry.
Beatrice Griffith (Title not yet announced.)
1946 *The House of Jacob,* by Jacquiline Margoliash.
Common Sense About Japan, by Helen Mears.

The John Day Foreign Service Prize

In honor of the twentieth anniversary of the American Foreign Service, John Day Co., Inc. announced in December 1944 a Foreign Service Book Contest. The competition was open only to members of the American Foreign Service — consuls, ministers and other civilian diplomatic personnel under the supervision of the State Department, or to the wife or husband of any of the foregoing. The award was $1,000, an outright prize of $500, the remainder to apply against book royalties. The contest, which closed on September 30, 1946, was open to fiction or non-fiction, on any subject of interest to the general reader. Other details may be obtained from the John Day Co., Inc., 40 East 49th Street, New York 17, N. Y.

The Alfred A. Knopf Literary Fellowships

To celebrate its twenty-fifth anniversary in 1939, Alfred A. Knopf, Inc., offered three annual awards of $1,200 for the purpose of assisting talented writers in completing planned, unfinished books.

The sums received under each fellowship are advances against royalties to be earned by the book and are payable in monthly installments. In all cases, American topics or themes are preferred.

In 1946 the fellowship program was revised to provide for four awards in three fields of literary achievement: (1) American history or biography; (2) Physical or biological science; (3) Fiction. Two awards are available in the first category—one of $5,000 and one of $2,500. The awards for science and fiction are $2,500 each.

Further details may be obtained from Alfred A. Knopf., Inc., 501 Madison Ave., New York 22, N. Y.

1940 Biography: *Commodore Vanderbilt: An Epic of the Steam Age,* by Dr. Wheaton J. Lane.
Fiction: *Days Are As Grass,* by Wallace Kelly.
History: *Airways: The History of Commercial Aviation in the United States,* by Henry Ladd Smith.

1941   Fiction: *Reunion at Strawberry Hill*, by Berenice Du Rae Thorpe.

       History: *A History of American Political Parties*, by Wilfred Binkley.

1942   Biography: *George Bancroft: Brahmin Rebel*, by Russell Blaine Nye.

       Fiction: *Bright Is the Morning*, by Robert Faucett Gibbons.

       History: *Prairie City*, by Dr. Angie Deboe.

1943   Biography: *No Man Knows My History*, by Fawn McKay Brodie.

       History: *History of the Modern American Navy*, by Donald W. Mitchell.

1944   Biography: *The Yankee Spirit*, by Stearns Morse.

       History: *A History of Country Life in America*, by Edward Townsend Booth.

1945   Biography: No award.

       Fiction: No award:

       History: *Men and Ideas in American Politics*, by Dr. Richard Hofstadter.
                    The Old Northwest, 1815-1840, by Dr. R. Carlyle Buley. (Divided award.)

       Science: No award.

McGraw-Hill Nursing Award

In 1945 the McGraw-Hill Book Company announced a contest for three outstanding manuscripts on nursing subjects. First prize, $1,000; second, $400; third, $100. The contest was open to any nurse in any country and to persons in other professional fields for a manuscript written in the English language concerning some aspect of nursing. The contest closed September 20, 1946. Complete details may be secured from John S. Crossman, manager and editor of the Health Education Department of the McGraw-Hill Book Company, 330 West 42nd Street, New York 18, N. Y.

The Macmillan Centenary Awards for the Armed Forces

In 1943 the Macmillan Company in England, Canada and the United States celebrated its centenary by offering a number of literary awards available to men and women under thirty-five years of age, serving in any branch of the armed forces of the United Nations. The principal awards consisted of $2,500 for the best novel, $2,500 for the best work of non-fiction, and smaller awards totalling $5,000 for other manuscripts. Prizes of similar value were offered in England.

AMERICAN PRIZES

1945 Fiction: *Not in Our Stars,* by Josiah E. Greene. American winner.
Desert Episode, by George C. Greenfield. British winner.
Non-fiction: *Democracy Needs the Negro,* by Spencer Logan.
American winner.
Lower Deck, by John Davies. British winner.

The Julian Messner Award

In 1945 Julian Messner, Inc., offered a total prize of $6,500,
including royalties, for the best book combatting racial or reli-
gious intolerance in America. The prize was offered for an unpublished novel, biography, history, play, poem, essay, pictorial
presentation, or scientific work effectively combatting growing
prejudices in America.

The contest closed August 15, 1946 and the winning manuscript will be published in the spring of 1947 by Julian Messner,
Inc., 8 West 40th Street, New York 18, N. Y.

Norton Medical Award

An annual prize of $3,500 is offered by W. W. Norton and
Company to encourage the writing of books on medicine and the
medical profession for the layman. The competition is open to
professional workers in the field of medicine or to writers col-
laborating with professional workers. The subject matter may be
autobiography, biography, history, or exposition of medical
science, research or theory. The manuscript must be written for
the layman. Of the $3,500 award, $1,000 is an outright grant,
the remainder is an advance against royalties. Details of the contest may be obtained from W. W. Norton & Company, Inc.,
70 Fifth Ave., New York 11, N. Y.

1945 *The Doctor's Job,* by Dr. Carl Binger.
1946 *Doctors East, Doctors West,* by Edward H. Hume.

Parents' Magazine Medal

The *Parents' Magazine* Medal is awarded annually to the
author of the year's most outstanding book for parents. The winning book is selected by a committee of distinguished authorities
in the field of parent education.

1927 *The Problem of Childhood,* by Angelo Patri. (Appleton-Century.)
1928 *Everyday Problems of the Everyday Child,* by Douglas A. Thom.
(Appleton-Century.)
1929 *Infancy and Human Growth,* by Arnold Gesell. (Macmillan.)

LITERARY PRIZES

1930 *Parents and the Preschool Child,* by William E. Blatz and Helen Bott. (Morrow.)

1931 *The Management of Young Children,* by William E. Blatz and Helen Bott. (Morrow.)

1932 *Home Guidance for Young Children,* by Grace Langdon. (John Day.)

1933 *Our Children,* by Sidonie Matsner Gruenberg and Dorothy Canfield Fisher. (Viking.)

1934 *Motion Pictures and Youth,* by the Payne Fund and the Motion Picture Research Council. (Macmillan.)

1935 *New Patterns in Sex Teaching,* by Frances Bruce Strain. (Appleton-Century.)

1936 *Parents Look at Modern Education,* by Winifred E. Bain. (Appleton-Century.)

1937 *Family Behavior,* by Bess V. Cunningham. (Saunders.)

1938 *The Nursery Years,* by Susan Isaacs. (Vanguard.)

1939 *We, The Parents,* by Sidonie M. Gruenberg. (Harper.)

1940 *Children in the Family,* by Florence Powdermaker and Louise Ireland Grimes. (Farrar & Rinehart.)
Your Child's Development and Guidance, by Lois Hayden Meek. (Lippincott.)

1941 *The Parents' Manual,* by Anna W. M. Wolf. (Simon & Schuster.)

1942 *Our Children Face War,* by Anna W. M. Wolf. (Houghton Mifflin.)
You, Your Children and the War, by Dorothy W. Baruch. (Appleton-Century.)

1943 *Our Young Folks,* by Dorothy Canfield Fisher. (Harcourt, Brace.)
Infant and Child in the Culture of Today, by Arnold Gesell and Frances L. Ilg. (Harper.)

1944 *Soldier to Civilian,* by Dr. George K. Pratt. (Whittlesey House.)

1945 No award.

Prentice-Hall and *Sewanee Review* Contest

Prentice-Hall and *The Sewanee Review* sponsored, in 1945, a $1,500 literary prize contest in memory of John Peale Bishop. Awards were made for the best essay, the best poem and the best piece of short fiction. The poetry and fiction divisions of the contest were open to Southern authors only. The essay division was open to any American citizen, but only essays dealing with Southern topics were eligible for consideration. The awards were: $200 for the winning essay; $200 for the winning piece of short fiction; $100 for the best poem. The sum of $1,000 was set aside as an advance against royalties and was divided equally among the winners.

Essay: *William Faulkner's Legend of the South,* by Malcolm Cowley.
Short Story: *The Guide,* by Andrew Lytle.
Poem: *Marchen,* by Randall Jarrell.

AMERICAN PRIZES

Reynal and Hitchcock Prizes

REYNAL AND HITCHCOCK NON-FICTION PRIZE

In 1940 Reynal and Hitchcock offered a prize of $2,500 for a book-length manuscript by a member of an American college or university staff. The award was offered for a book written for the general reader, not a textbook or professional book—"a really original and distinguished piece of work covering a field of serious interest."

1941 *The Destiny of Western Man,* by W. T. Stace. (Reynal & Hitchcock.)

"YOUTH TODAY" CONTEST

The new children's book department of Reynal and Hitchcock, Inc., sponsored a $3,500 "Youth Today" contest in 1945. The competition accepted manuscripts from new or established authors dealing in a sensitive, realistic manner with "some aspect of contemporary American life and youth problems, either fiction, or non-fiction." The award was offered for "a story intimately related to our modern world, of interest to young readers, and vitalized by the author's genuine concern with an important problem of young people today." Reynal and Hitchcock, Inc., offered the prize to "stimulate the writing of books that add to the understanding, sympathy and wisdom with which young people look at the age in which we live."

1946 *Willow Hill,* by Phyllis Whitney.

Rinehart and Company Scholarships

In 1945 Farrar and Rinehart awarded two scholarships designed to enable young writers to devote full time to study and writing under skilled supervision. The scholarships, which provided an outright prize of $1,000 each, were given in honor of Du Bose Heyward and Stephen Vincent Benét. The scholarship program was taken over by Rinehart and Company in 1946.

1945 *Narrow the Heart,* by Margaret Anne Morgan.
The Changeling, by Roy Flynn.

Saturday Review of Literature Special Award

The editors of the *Saturday Review of Literature* have, from time to time, conferred a special Award for Distinguished Service to American Literature. The award consists of a plaque bearing an inscription and a hand-carved depiction of a rooster, the masthead design of the *Saturday Review of Literature*. The award is made only when, in the opinion of the editors, someone or something really contributes to the development of the culture of America.

1940 "Information Please", radio program.
1941 Ellen Glasgow, novelist.
1944 *Yank, the Army Weekly.*
1945 The Council on Books in Wartime for its *Armed Services Editions.* Duplicate award to Philip Van Doren Stern, manager of the *Armed Services Editions.*
1946 Irving Berlin for *This is the Army.*

Scribner Prize in American History

In commemoration of the 100th anniversary of the firm, Charles Scribner's Sons offered a prize of $10,000 for a manuscript of major importance in the field of American history. Of the $10,000 prize, $5,000 was an outright prize, and $5,000 an advance on account of royalties. The competition was held under the auspices of The Society of American Historians, which selected the judges. In considering the manuscripts, the judges looked for the obvious qualities of literary and historical merit, but also for its interest to the general reader. The purpose of the prize, in the words of the sponsor, was "to make history readable." The contest closed February 1, 1946 and the winner was announced on November 7, 1946.

1946 *Ordeal of the Union,* by Allan Nevins.

Simon and Schuster Fellowship Fund

In 1945 the editors of Simon and Schuster set aside a fund of $50,000 for the purpose of aiding young novelists. Any writer under thirty-eight is eligible, providing he has no previous commitment for novels to another publisher and providing he submits material of talent and promise to the editors. The sums paid to individuals vary and are dependent upon the circumstances under which the books are being written. There is no limit to the number of applicants in any one year, and no blanket formula is to be used in judging. The plan of assistance will be worked out on the basis of material and information supplied by the candidates. Simon and Schuster reserves the right to decide whether or not the completed book will be published.

The fund will be kept revolving with the aid of profits accruing to Simon and Schuster from the books published. The plan will be given a three years' trial, then reviewed; if it is found successful, it will be continued.

1945 *Aurora Dawn*, by Herman Wouk.
   Time Is My Enemy, by Marian Minus.
   The Phantom Year, by Jane Albrecht.
   The House in the Barrel, by Eli Waldron.
1946 *When the Treetops Sing*, by Genevieve Lowry.

Westminster Annual Award For Fiction

In 1945 the Westminster Press announced an annual prize for fiction, with a $5,000 award for the best novel emphasizing the influence of Christian faith in contemporary life or history. No restriction is placed upon setting, situation, or characters; every manuscript submitted will be judged solely on the basis of literary merit. Because no award was made in 1946, the prize in 1947 will amount to $8,000. Full information is available upon request to the Westminster Annual Award, 952 Witherspoon Building, Philadelphia 7, Pennsylvania.

1946 No award.

Whittlesey House Fifteenth Anniversary Fellowship Awards

In celebration of their fifteenth anniversary, Whittlesey House, a division of the McGraw-Hill Book Company, and *Science Illustrated* established in 1945 a program of fellowship awards in science to encourage competent authors to write on scientific subjects for the layman. In addition to the first prize of $10,000, $1,000 was offered to the author of each project accepted for publication, in order to enable the author to complete his project and to do research otherwise impossible. Information concerning the competition, which closed November 1, 1946, may be obtained from Whittlesey House, 330 West 42nd Street, New York 18, N. Y.

JUVENILE PRIZES
The Caldecott Medal

The Caldecott Medal, first awarded in 1938, is presented annually by the same committee awarding the John Newbery Medal. The donor is Frederic G. Melcher, editor of *Publishers' Weekly*. The winning book must be first published in America, but the artist need not be an American citizen. This was the first award given in recognition of the illustrator of a book.

The award was named for Randolph Caldecott, the famous English illustrator, who died in St. Augustine in 1886. He, together with Kate Greenaway and Walter Crane, began a new era of picture books for children. On the face of the medal is a reproduction of Caldecott's original illustration of John Gilpin on his famous ride. The reverse side carries an illustration of "four and twenty blackbirds baked in a pie". Around the central engraving is the inscription, "For the most distinguished American Picture Book for Children", with space for the name of the recipient and the date. The sculptor was René Chambellan, who designed the Newbery Medal.

1938 *Animals of the Bible*, illustrated by Dorothy Lathrop. Text selected by Helen Dean Fish from the King James Bible. (Stokes.)

1939 *Mei Li*, written and illustrated by Thomas Handforth. (Doubleday.)

1940 *Abraham Lincoln*, written and illustrated by Ingri and Edgar d'Aulaire. (Doubleday.)

1941 *They Were Strong and Good*, written and illustrated by Robert Lawson. (Doubleday.)

1942 *Make Way for Ducklings*, written and illustrated by Robert McCloskey. (Viking.)

1943 *The Little House*, written and illustrated by Virginia Lee Burton. (Houghton.) ..

1944 *Many Moons*, illustrated by Louis Slobodkin, written by James Thurber. (Harcourt.)

1945 *Prayer for a Child*, illustrated by Elizabeth Orton Jones, written by Rachel Field. (Macmillan.)

1946 *The Rooster Crows*, written and illustrated by Maud and Miska Petersham. (Macmillan.)

Child Study Association Award

The Children's Book Committee of the Child Study Association of America offers an annual honorary award to a book for children dealing in a realistic manner with contemporary problems. The winner is selected from among the year's publications by the Children's Book Committee. The award has been made annually in the Fall since 1943.

1943 *Keystone Kids,* by John R. Tunis. (Harcourt.)
1944 *The House,* by Marjorie Hill Alee. (Houghton.)
1945 *The Moved Outers,* by Florence Crannell Means. (Houghton.)

Downey Award

Pro Parvulis Book Club, the national book club for Catholic children, inaugurated in 1942 an annual award of a silver medal, the Downey Award, for "the finest American children's book written in the Catholic tradition." It was established in memory of the late Father Francis X. Downey, founder of the Pro Parvulis Book Club.

1942 *The Red Hat,* by Covelle Newcomb. (Longmans, Green.)
1943 *Rathina,* by Marin Cregan. (Macmillan.)
1944 *The Secret of Pooduck Island,* by Alfred Noyes. (Lippincott-Stokes.)
1945 No award.

Julia Ellsworth Ford Foundation Prize

This Foundation was established by Julia Ellsworth Ford in 1934 for the purpose of "encouraging originality and imagination in children's literature in the United States." The prize is awarded annually for a juvenile manuscript. Originally the amount of $1,450 was divided into several awards. Since that time the amount of the prize has varied; in 1945 it was a single prize of $1,250. The several winners for the years 1935 and 1936 can be found in the 1939 edition of *Famous Literary Prizes and Their Winners.* The contest is open to all authors and the prize-winning manuscript is selected by a board of well-known authorities on children's books. Further information may be obtained from the Julia Ellsworth Ford Foundation, in care of Julian Messner, Inc., 8 West 40th Street, New York 18, N. Y.

1937 *My Brother Was Mozart,* by Benson Wheeler and Claire Lee Purdy. Illustrated by Theodore Nadejen. (Holt.)
      The Stage-Struck Seal, by James Hull. Illustrated by the author. (Holt.)
1938 *"Hello, the Boat!",* by Phyllis Crawford. Illustrated by Edward Laning. (Holt.)
1939 *Falcon, Fly Back,* by Elinore Blaisdell. Illustrated by the author. (Messner.)
1940 *The Listening Man,* by Lucy Embury. Illustrated by Russel Hamilton. (Messner.)
1941 *Walt Whitman, Builder for America,* by Babette Deutsch. Illustrated by Rafaello Busoni. (Messner.)

1942 *Journey Cake,* by Isabel McLennan McMeekin. Illustrated by Nicholas Panesis. (Messner.)

1943 *Valiant Minstrel: The Story of Harry Lauder,* by Gladys Malvern. Illustrated by Corinne Malvern. (Messner.)

1944 *Raymond L. Ditmars: His Exciting Career with Reptiles, Insects and Animals,* by Laura Newbold Wood. (Messner.)

1945 *The Wonderful Year, by* Nancy Barnes. Illustrated by Kate Seredy. (Messner.)

1946 *A Horse to Remember,* by Genevieve Torrey Eames. (Messner.)

Junior Scholastic Magazine Gold Seal Award

The *Junior Scholastic* Gold Seal Award is given at irregular intervals to those juvenile books "that are considered to be an enriching experience in the lives of young Americans." The seal is of stiff gold paper, designed to be pasted on the prize-winning book; it is about an inch and a half in diameter and carries the inscription: "Awarded—*Junior Scholastic Magazine*—Gold Seal". The first Gold Seal Awards were made in 1942.

1942 *Paul Bunyan,* by Esther Shephard, illustrated by Rockwell Kent. (Harcourt.)
Indian Captive, by Lois Lenski. (Stokes.)
Citadel of a Hundred Stairways, by Alida Sims Malkus. (Winston.)
The Mayos, by Adolph Regli. (Messner.)
Shooting Star, by William E. Wilson. (Farrar & Rinehart.)
I Have Just Begun to Fight, by Edward Ellsberg. (Dodd.)
Adam of the Road, by Elizabeth Janet Gray. (Viking.)
Goethals of the Panama Canal, by Howard Fast. (Messner.)
Snow Treasure, by Marie McSwigan. (Dutton.)
Dragon Ship, by William S. Resnick. (Coward-McCann.)

1943 *Tom Whipple,* by Walter D. Edmonds. (Dodd.)
Gift of the Forest, by Reginald Lal Singh and Eloise Lownsbery. (Longmans.)
Struggle Is Our Brother, by Gregor Felsen. (Dutton.)
Walter Reed, by Laura Newbold Wood. (Messner.)
We'll Meet in England, by Kitty Barne. (Dodd.)
Submarine Sailor, by Gregor Felsen. (Dutton.)
Hosh-Ki the Navajo, by Florence Hayes. (Random.)

1944 *Yankee Thunder,* by Irwin Shapiro. (Messner.)
The Good Ship Red Lily, by Constance Savery. (Longmans.)
Giants of China, by Helena Kuo. (Dutton.)

1945 *Nathan Hale, Patriot,* by Martha Mann. (Dodd.)
The Land of the Chinese People, by Cornelia Spencer. (Lippincott.)
Sentinel of the Snow Peaks, by Harold McCracken. (Lippincott.)

1946 *Justin Morgan Had a Horse,* by Marguerite Henry. (Wilcox & Follett.)

LITERARY PRIZES
The John Newbery Medal

The John Newbery Medal has been awarded annually since 1922 by the Children's Library Association of the Division of Libraries for Children and Young People of the American Library Association for the most distinguished contribution to literature for American children. Books by authors of foreign birth are eligible if the books are first published in America. Compilations are not eligible.

The announcement of this award, which is for a book of the previous year, is made at the Annual Conference of the American Library Association, usually held in June. The Committee which makes the award now consists of twenty-three members — the Chairman, the four officers of the Children's Library Association, the chairman of the previous year, the chairman and four members of the Book Evaluation Committee, the chairman of the other four standing committees, three members-at-large, and the chairman and four members of the School Library Section. The bronze medal is the gift of Frederic G. Melcher, editor of the *Publishers' Weekly*. The design for the medal was made by the American sculptor, René Chambellan.

This prize for the best juvenile is most appropriately named for John Newbery (1713-1767), a London bookseller, who first conceived the idea of publishing books expressly for children. Newbery's famous Juvenile Library was made up of tiny volumes, four inches tall, bound in "flowery and gilt" Dutch paper.

A more detailed description of Newbery's publishing activities may be found in the 1939 edition of *Famous Literary Prizes and Their Winners*.

1922   *The Story of Mankind,* by Hendrik Willem van Loon. Illustrated by the author. (Liveright; Garden City.)

1923   *The Voyages of Doctor Dolittle,* by Hugh Lofting. Illustrated by the author. (Stokes.)

1924   *The Dark Frigate,* by Charles Boardman Hawes. (Little.)

1925   *Tales From Silver Lands,* by Charles Joseph Finger. Illustrated by Paul Honoré. (Doubleday.)

1926   *Shen of the Sea,* by Arthur Bowie Chrisman. Illustrated by Else Hasselriis. (Dutton.)

1927   *Smoky: the Cowhorse,* by Will James. Illustrated by the author. (Scribner.)

1928   *Gay Neck,* by Dhan Gopal Mukerji. Illustrated by Boris Artzybasheff. (Dutton.)

AMERICAN PRIZES

1929 *The Trumpeter of Krakow,* by Eric P. Kelly. Illustrated by Angela Pruszynska. (Macmillan.)

1930 *Hitty,* by Rachel Field. Illustrated by Dorothy Lathrop. (Macmillan.)

1931 *The Cat Who Went to Heaven,* by Elizabeth Coatsworth. Illustrated by Lynd Ward. (Macmillan.)

1932 *Waterless Mountain,* by Laura Adams Armer. Illustrated by the the author, and her husband, Sidney Armer. (Longmans.)

1933 *Young Fu of the Upper Yangtze,* by Elizabeth Foreman Lewis. Illustrated by Kurt Wiese. (Winston.)

1934 *Invincible Louisa,* by Cornelia Meigs. (Little.)

1935 *Dobry,* by Monica Shannon. Illustrated by Atanas Katchamakoff. (Viking.)

1936 *Caddie Woodlawn,* by Carol Ryrie Brink. Illustrated by Kate Seredy. (Macmillan).

1937 *Roller Skates,* by Ruth Sawyer. Illustrated by Valenti Angelo. (Viking.)

1938 *The White Stag,* by Kate Seredy. Illustrated by the author. (Viking.)

1939 *Thimble Summer,* by Elizabeth Enright. Illustrated by the author. (Farrar & Rinehart.)

1940 *Daniel Boone,* by James Daugherty. Illustrated by the author. (Viking.)

1941 *Call It Courage,* by Armstrong Sperry. Illustrated by the author. (Macmillan.)

1942 *The Matchlock Gun,* by Walter D. Edmonds. Illustrated by Paul Lantz. (Dodd.)

1943 *Adam of the Road,* by Elizabeth Janet Gray. Illustrated by Robert Lawson. (Viking.)

1944 *Johnny Tremain,* by Esther Forbes. Illustrated by Lynd Ward. (Houghton.)

1945 *Rabbit Hill,* by Robert Lawson. Illustrated by the author. (Viking.)

1946 *Strawberry Girl,* by Lois Lenski. Illustrated by the author. (Lippincott.)

For complete descriptions of the first twelve Newbery books see *The Newbery Medal Books 1922-1933: Their Authors, Illustrators and Publishers,* by Muriel E. Cann. Published by the Public Library, Boston.

New York *Herald-Tribune* Children's Spring Book Festival Awards

In 1937 two awards of $250 each were established by the New York *Herald-Tribune* for the best books for younger children and for older children published between January and June. In 1941 the system of awards was revised. Three awards, of $200 each, are given to the best books in the following three classes: young children, middle-age children, and other children. Each year a jury, composed of distinguished experts in the field of juvenile literature, is chosen to make the selections.

1937 *Seven Simeons*, by Boris Artzybasheff. For younger children. Illustrated by the author. (Viking.)
The Smuggler's Sloop, by Robb White III. For older children. Illustrated by Andrew Wyeth. (Little.)

1938 *The Hobbit*, by J. R. Tolkien. For younger children. Illustrated by the author. (Houghton.)
The Iron Duke, by John R. Tunis. For older children. Illustrated by Johan Bull. (Harcourt.)

1939 *The Story of Horace*, by Alice M. Coats. For younger children. Illustrated by the author. (Coward.)
The Hired Man's Elephant, by Phil Stong. For older children. Illustrated by Doris Lee. (Dodd.)

1940 *That Mario*, by Lucy Herndon Crockett. For younger children. Illustrated by the author. (Holt.)
Cap'n Ezra, Privateer, by James D. Adams. For older children. Illustrated by I. B. Hazelton. (Harcourt.)

1941 *In My Mother's House*, by Ann Nolan Clark. For younger children. Illustrated by Velino Herrera. (Viking.)
Pete, by Tom Robinson. For middle-age children. Illustrated by Morgan Dennis. (Viking.)
Clara Barton. by Mildren Mastin Pace. For older children. (Scribner.)

1942 *Mr. Tootwhistle's Invention*, by Peter Wells. For younger children. Illustrated by the author. (Winston.)
I Have Just Begun to Fight: The Story of John Paul Jones, by Commander Edward Ellsberg. For middle-age children. Illustrated by Gerald Foster. (Dodd.)
None But the Brave, by Rosamond Van der Zee Marshall. For older children. Illustrated by Gregor Duncan. (Houghton.)

1943 *Five Golden Wrens*, by Hugh Troy. For younger children. Illustrated by the author. (Oxford.)
These Happy Golden Years, by Laura Ingalls Wilder. For middle-age children. Illustrated by Helen Sewell and Mildred Boyle. (Harper.)
Patterns on the Wall, by Elizabeth Yates. For older children. (Knopf.)

1944 *A Ring and a Riddle*, by M. Ilin and E. Segal. For younger children. Illustrated by Vera Bock. (Lippincott.)
They Put Out to Sea, by Roger Duvoisin. For middle-age children. Illustrated by the author. (Knopf.)
Storm Canvas, by Armstrong Sperry, For older children. Illustrated by the author. (Winston.)

1945 *Little People in a Big Country*, by Norma Cohn. For younger children. Illustrated by Tashkent Children's Art Training Center in Soviet Uzbekistan. (Oxford.)
Gulf Stream, by Ruth Brindze. Illustrated by Helene Carter. For middle-age children. (Vanguard.)
Sandy, by Elizabeth Janet Gray. For older children. (Viking.)

1946 *Farm Stories.* Award divided between Gustaf Tenggren, illustrator, and Kathryn and Byron Jackson, authors. For younger children. (Simon & Schuster.)
The Thirteenth Stone, by Jean Bothwell, illustrated by Margaret Ayer. For middle-age children. (Harcourt.)
The Quest of the Golden Condor, by Clayton Knight. Illustrated by the author. For older children. (Knopf.)

Pacific Northwest Young Reader's Choice Award

The Pacific Northwest Library Association presents an annual award to the author of a recent book which has proved popular with boys and girls from the fourth to eighth grades. Originally the book was chosen from a poll of children's librarians of the Pacific Northwest. Later this policy was changed and the winner is now selected by direct vote of grade school children.

1940 *Paul Bunyan Swings His Axe,* by Dell J. McCormick. (Caxton.)
1941 *Mr. Popper's Penguins,* by Florence and Richard Atwater. (Little.)
1942 *By the Shores of Silver Lake,* by Laura Ingalls Wilder. (Harper.)
1943 *Lassie Come-Home,* by Eric Knight. (Winston.)
1944 *Black Stallion,* by Walter Farley. (Random.)
1945 *Snow Treasure,* by Marie McSwigan. (Dutton.)
1946 *Return of Silver Chief,* by John S. O'Brien. (Winston.)

Youth Today Contest

See Publishers' Prizes, Reynal & Hitchcock, page 53.

POETRY PRIZES

Academy of American Poets Award

The Academy of American Poets, 435 East 52nd Street, New York, N. Y., sets forth its purpose as twofold: "first, to encourage and foster the work of American poets of proven gifts and merit; second, to discover new poetic genius wherever it may be in America." The Academy plans to offer an annual Fellowship of $5,000 to a deserving American poet who, for practical reasons, cannot otherwise devote himself entirely to the writing of poetry. Fellowships may be awarded to the same individual for successive years without limit.

In 1937, Edwin Markham was given a special award of $5,000 for great achievement in poetry. This was the first award since the Academy was chartered in 1934. The first formal Fellowship was awarded in 1946.

1946   Edgar Lee Masters.

Harriet Monroe Poetry Award

The Harriet Monroe Poetry Award of $500 was established under the will of Harriet Monroe, founder and for more than twenty years editor of *Poetry, A Magazine of Verse,* for the advancement and encouragement of poetry. It is administered by the University of Chicago and is to be awarded from time to time to an American poet of distinction and distinguished service. Preference is given to poets of progressive rather than academic tendencies.

1941   Muriel Rukeyser   1945   Marianne Moore
1944   Marianne Moore   1946   Wallace Stevens

League to Support Poetry

The League to Support Poetry, 327 West 18th Street, New York, N. Y., was founded in 1936 for the purpose of publishing distinguished volumes of poetry on a self-supporting basis which would allow royalties to be paid to their authors. All the books which the League has already published, with the endorsement of the member-groups and judges, were financed by advance subscription. The League publishes one volume of poetry, on a royalty basis, every October. The book of the year is chosen by a competition, open to all poets, which is held during January and February of each year. The winner is announced in May. The following volumes have been published:

1940 *Core of Fire*, by Kenneth Slade Alling.
1941 *Hawk's Way*, by Ted Olson.
1942 *Heavenly Body*, by Starr Nelson.
     Rock and Cumulus, by Richard Leon Spain.
1943 *Louder Than the Drum*, by Gerard Previn Meyer.
1944 *There Is Still Time*, by Carolyn Wilson Link.
1945 *Brief Enterprise*, by Alice Monks Mears.
1946 *Parade of Doves*, by Eve Triem.

Poetry Magazine Awards

Poetry, A Magazine of Verse, published at 232 East Erie Street, Chicago, Illinois, sponsors eight awards annually. The prizes are given for work that has appeared in the magazine during the preceding year and are announced in the November issue of the magazine. In each case, the award winners listed below include only those since 1938. Previous winners may be found in the 1939 edition of *Famous Literary Prizes and Their Winners*. Many names, later to become prominent in the history of American poetry, first achieved recognition in *Poetry*. The long list of winners of the prizes listed below includes such famous American poets as Carl Sandburg, Vachel Lindsay, Robert Frost, Edwin Arlington Robinson, Elinor Wylie, Hart Crane, Edna St. Vincent Millay, Marianne Moore, Robert Penn Warren, William Carlos Williams, and W. H. Auden.

EDWARD BLAND MEMORIAL FELLOWSHIP PRIZE

This prize of $50, formerly known as the Fellowship Prize, was founded in 1943 through the generosity of the Chicago Poets' Class, a group of young Negro poets. It is given preferably for a work "which most profoundly contributes to or expresses understanding and contact between nations, races, classes, or creeds."

1943 Patrick Anderson.
1944 Oscar Williams.
1945 May Sarton.

OSCAR BLUMENTHAL PRIZE

This prize of $100, founded in 1936, is awarded annually by Charles M. Leviton in memory of Oscar Blumenthal.

1936	Marion Strobel.	1941	Stanley J. Kunitz.
1937	Thomas Hornsby Ferril.	1942	E. L. Mayo.
1938	Dylan Thomas.	1943	John Ciardi.
1939	Maxwell Bodenheim.	1944	P. K. Page.
1940	Muriel Rukeyser.	1945	Yvor Winters.

AMERICAN PRIZES

FIRST APPEARANCE PRIZE

This prize was founded in 1945 for a poem or group of poems published in *Poetry*, marking the author's first appearance in the magazine. The award, given anonymously, is a $50 bond.

1945 Louis Coxe.

GUARANTORS PRIZE

This prize of $100, founded in 1913, is financed by the Friday Club of Chicago.

1939	Stephen Spender.	1943	John Frederick Nims.
1940	Kenneth Fearing.	1944	F. R. Scott.
1941	Paul Engle.	1945	Ray Smith.
1942	St. - J. Perse.		

LEVINSON PRIZE

This prize was founded in 1914 and is awarded for a poem or group of poems by an American citizen. The prize is $100 and is given by the family of the late Salmon O. Levinson.

1939	E. E. Cummings.	1943	John Malcolm Brinnin.
1940	Robinson Jeffers.	1944	John Frederick Nims.
1941	Archibald MacLeish.	1945	Dylan Thomas.
1942	Karl J. Shapiro.		

HARRIET MONROE LYRIC PRIZE

A memorial prize of $100 is awarded for a lyric poem or group of lyric poems published in *Poetry* during the year preceding the the award. Marion Strobel is the donor of the award.

1937	Roger Roughton.	1942	John Frederick Nims.
1938	H. H. Lewis.	1943	H. B. Mallalieu.
1939	Malcolm Cowley.	1944	William Meredith.
1940	Louis MacNeice.	1945	Will Gibson.
1941	Frederic Prokosch.		

EUNICE TIETJENS MEMORIAL PRIZE

This award of $100, established in 1944, is a memorial to a former associate editor of *Poetry*. It is presented by Cloyd Head for a poem or group of poems by an American citizen.

1944 John Ciardi.
1945 Marie Borroff.

YOUNGER POETS PRIZE

This $100 prize, formerly the Jeannette Sewell Davis Prize, was established in 1934 to be awarded to a *young* poet.

LITERARY PRIZES

1934	Jesse Stuart.	1940	Robert Friend.
1935	No award.	1941	Karl J. Shapiro.
1936	David Schubert.	1942	Katinka Loeser.
1937	William Pillin.	1943	Randall Jarrell.
1938	D. S. Savage.	1944	Howard Moss.
1939	John Malcolm Brinnin.	1945	William Jay Smith.

Poetry Society of America Awards

POETRY SOCIETY ANNUAL AWARD

An annual award is made by the Poetry Society of America, 687 Lexington Ave., New York 22, N. Y. The recipients have been as follows:

1938 Helen Morrow and Oscar Williams.
1939 Helen Morrow and Harold Vinal.
1940 Clark Mills and Daniel Smythe.
1941 Frederick Wright and Rosalie Moore.
1942 Edith Henrich.
1943 Edith Henrich and Jane Dransfield.
1944 Rosalie Moore and Elma Dean.
1945 Elda Tanasso and Mary Sinton Leitch.

LOLA RIDGE MEMORIAL AWARD

An annual award of $100 is offered by S. A. DeWitt of New York through the Poetry Society of America.

1942 Elsa Barker.
1943 Norman Rosten and Margaret R. Richter.
1944 Alice Monks Mears.
1945 No award.
1946 Jules Alan Wein and Sidney Shanker.

THE SHELLEY MEMORIAL AWARD

An annual prize in memory of Percy Bysshe Shelley was donated by Mary P. Sears, who, in her will, left a trust fund of $20,000 to be known as the Shelley Memorial Fund and to be administered by the Old Colony Trust Company of Boston. The prize, approximately $800, is given to a living American poet, chosen on the basis of merit and need. The jury consists of three poets, one chosen by the president of Radcliffe College, one by the president of the University of California, and one by the governing board of the Poetry Society of America.

1930 Conrad Aiken.
1931 Lizette Reese.
1932 Archibald MacLeish.
1933 Stephen Vincent Benét.
1934 Frances Frost and Lola Ridge.
1935 Marya Zaturenska and Lola Ridge.
1936 Josephine Miles.
1937 Charlotte Wilder and Ben Belitt.
1938 Lincoln Fitzell.
1939 Robert Francis and Harry Brown.
1940 Herbert Brunchen and Winfield Townley Scott.
1941 Marianne Moore.
1942 Ridgely Torrence.
1943 Robert Penn Warren and Percy MacKaye.
1944 Edgar Lee Masters.
1945 E. E. Cummings.
1946 Karl Shapiro.

Pulitzer Prize

See General Prizes, page 31.

Yale Series of Younger Poets

These contests were initiated in 1919 by Clarence Day, well-known author and brother of the founder of Yale University Press. From 1920 to 1924, two volumes were published during each of the two yearly contests, held in the spring and fall. From 1924 to 1932 two volumes were issued semi-annually. In 1933, when Stephen Vincent Benét became editor of the Yale Series of Younger Poets, it was decided to issue only one volume a year. In 1946 Wystan Hugh Auden became editor, succeeding Archibald MacLeish. The contest closes on March first of each year.

The competition, which is designed to provide a publishing medium for the first volumes of America's promising poets, is open to American citizens under thirty who have not previously published a volume of verse. There is a prize of $100 in addition to the usual author's royalties and publication of the volume by the Yale University Press. The award of $100 was suggested by Stephen Vincent Benét and is paid out of the editor's fee.

Rules of the contest may be obtained from the Yale Series of Younger Poets, Yale University Press, New Haven, Connecticut.

1920 *The Tempering,* by Howard Buck.
Forgotten Shrines, by John Chipman Farrar.
Four Gardens, by David Osborne Hamilton.

Spires and Poplars, by Alfred Raymond Bellinger.
The White God and Other Poems, by Thomas Caldecot Chubb.
1921 *Where Lilith Dances,* by Darl Macleod Boyle.
Wild Geese, by Theodore H. Banks, Jr.
Horizons, by Viola C. White.
Wampum and Old Gold, by Hervey Allen.
The Golden Darkness, by Oscar Williams.
1922 *White April,* by Harold Vinal.
Dreams and a Sword, by Medora C. Addison.
Hidden Waters, by Bernard Raymund.
Attitudes, by Paul Tanaquil.
1923 *The Last Lutanist,* by Dean B. Lyman, Jr.
Battle-Retrospect, by Amos Niven Wilder.
Silver Wands, by Marion M .Boyd.
Mosaics, by Beatrice E. Harmon.
1924 *Up and Down,* by Elizabeth Jessup Blake.
1925 *Coach into Pumpkin,* by Dorothy E. Reid.
1926 *Quest,* by Eleanor Slater.
High Passage, by Thomas Hornsby Ferril.
1927 *Dark Pavilion,* by Lindley Williams Hubbell.
Twist o' Smoke, by Mildred Bowers.
1928 *A Stranger and Afraid,* by Ted Olson.
This Unchanging Mask, by Francis Claiborne Mason.
1929 *Hemlock Wall,* by Frances M. Frost.
Half-Light and Overtones, by Henri Faust.
1930 *Virtuosa: A Book of Verse,* by Louise Owen.
1931 *Dark Certainty,* by Dorothy Belle Flanagan.
1932 *Worn Earth,* by Paul H. Engle.
1933 *Dark Hills Under,* by Shirley Barker.
1934 *Permit Me Voyage,* by James Agee.
1935 *Theory of Flight,* by Murial Rukeyser.
1936 *The Deer Come Down,* by Edward Weismiller.
1937 *The Gardener Mind,* by Margaret Haley.
1938 *Letter to a Comrade,* by Joy Davidman.
1939 *The Connecticut River and Other Poems,* by Reuel Denney.
1940 *Return Again, Traveler,* by Norman Rosten.
1941 *The Metaphysical Sword,* by Jeremy Ingalls.
1942 *For My People,* by Margaret Walker.
1943 *Love Letter From an Impossible Land,* by William Meredith.
1944 *Cut Is the Branch,* by Charles E. Butler.
1945 *Family Circle,* by Eve Merriam.
1946 *Poems,* by Joan Vincent Murray.

DRAMA PRIZES
Sidney Howard Memorial Award

In 1939 the five directors of the Playwrights' Company, Maxwell Anderson, S. N. Behrman, Elmer Rice, Robert E. Sherwood and John F. Wharton, established the Sidney Howard Memorial Award of $1,500. The prize, a memorial to Sidney Howard, who was a Playwrights' Company director, is given annually to a new American playwright who, with no previous noteworthy success in the theater, has shown talent through the production of one or more of his plays in New York. The award is not designed to honor the "best play of the season," but to give support to a promising playwright. In 1941 the Playwrights' Company, unable to agree upon a recipient for the award, donated the prize money to the Authors' League Fund of the Authors' League of America for financial assistance to needy young dramatists. In 1943 the directors deviated slightly from the rules and awarded the prize money to the New School for Social Research to enable that group to produce *Winter Soldiers,* by Dan James.

1940   *Thunder Rock,* by Robert Ardrey. (Dramatists.)
1941-1944   No awards. See above.
1945   *The Glass Menagerie,* by Tennessee Williams. (Random.)
1946   *Born Yesterday,* by Garson Kanin. (Viking.)
      Home of the Brave, by Arthur Laurents. (Random.)

New York Drama Critics Circle Award

In 1935 the play reviewers of New York established an organization known as the New York Drama Critics Circle. The Circle awards a Medal each season to an American playwright for the best play, in the Circle opinion, produced in New York City. The prize is a silver plaque depicting a scene from the old John Street Theater. This award was established to offset the Pulitzer Drama Award with which the critics are rarely in agreement. In 1938 the Circle initiated an award for the best foreign play of the season. In both cases the Circle withholds the award if no play is deemed worthy of the distinction.

1936   *Winterset,* by Maxwell Anderson. (Dodd.)
1937   *High Tor,* by Maxwell Anderson. (Dodd.)
1938   *Of Mice and Men,* by John Steinbeck. (Covici.)
      Shadow and Substance, by Paul Vincent Carroll. (Random.)
1939   No award for American play.
      The White Steed, by Paul Vincent Carroll. (Random.)

[71]

1940 *The Time of Your Life,* by William Saroyan. (Harcourt.)
No award for foreign play.
1941 *The Watch on the Rhine,* by Lillian Hellman. (Random.)
The Corn Is Green, by Emlyn Williams. (Random.)
1942 No award for American play.
Blithe Spirit, by Noel Coward. (Doubleday.)
1943 *The Patriots,* by Sidney Kingsley. (Random.)
No award for foreign play.
1944 No award for American play.
Jacobowsky and the Colonel, by Franz Werfel and S. N. Behrman. (Random.)
1945 *The Glass Menagerie,* by Tennessee Williams. (Random.)
No award for foreign play.
1946 No awards given.

Pulitzer Prize

See General Prizes, page 29.

Charles H. Sergel Award

This award, established by Annie Meyers Sergel in memory of her husband, Charles H. Sergel, founder of the Dramatic Publishing Company of Chicago, is designed to encourage the writing of new American plays. The award is administered by the University of Chicago. The competition was originally conducted annually, with a prize of $500. In 1942-43, it was decided to give the award every two years, with a prize of $1,000. The contest is open to any citizen of the United States for a full-length original play. Further information may be obtained from the Charles H. Sergel Play Contest, University of Chicago.

1938 *The Boar,* by Rosalie Moore.
1939 *Ring One for Central,* by Carl Allenworth.
1940 *Prelude to '76,* by Robert Whitehand.
1941 *When the Time Comes,* by Harry Kleiner.
1942-43 *Candle to the Sun,* by Lewis Beach.
1944-45 *The River,* by Bob Stuart McKnight.

Stanford University Awards

The Dramatists' Alliance of Stanford University, an association of faculty and alumni interested non-professionally in drama, offers several drama awards at regular intervals.

ALDEN AWARD

This award, in memory of Raymond MacDonald Alden, writer and teacher of Stanford University, is offered for a one-act play.

AMERICAN PRIZES

The prize of $50 is given every two years, alternating with the Stephen Vincent Benét Award.

1941 *Until Charlot Comes Home,* by Rachel Reynolds.
1942 *Ballad Requiem for Lincoln,* by M. Greenwald.
1943 *Home Is the Hunter,* by Alice M. Dennis.
1945 *Summer Fury,* by James Broughton.

MAXWELL ANDERSON AWARD

The Maxwell Anderson Award of $100 for verse drama was established at Stanford University in 1936 in honor of the foremost dramatic poet of America, who was once a graduate student at the University. The aim of the contest is to encourage the production of good plays in verse on American themes. The contest is open to all persons interested in dramatic composition, without regard to training or experience. No play is acceptable if it has been produced in any theater or if it has been offered previously for this award. There are no restrictions as to theme, verse-form, or length; one-act plays are eligible. Since 1943, the award alternated with the Stevens Award for prose drama.

Information may be obtained from the Proctor of the Maxwell Anderson Contest, Office 200M, Stanford University, California.

1936 *Surrey,* by Florette Henri.
1937 *Souvenir de la Malmaison,* by Dorothy Dow.
1938 *John Brown,* by Kirke Mechem.
1939 *Night Before the Border,* by Jean Clark.
1940 *A Parting at Imsdorf,* by N. Richard Nusbaum.
1941 *The Levite,* by Agnes Irene Smith.
1942 *Night Song,* by Howard Richardson. (This play ran in New York under the title, *Dark of the Moon.)*
1944 *Lead Her Up to Candy,* by Donald Lawhon Stofle.
1946 No award.

MILES McKINNON ANDERSON AWARD

In 1945 a new prize was offered in memory of Miles McKinnon Anderson. The award of $100 is for a full-length prose drama "showing the sturdy constructive qualities of daily life in the North American scene." This award alternates with the Etherege Award.

1946 *The Festered Lily,* by Hermine Duthie.

STEPHEN VINCENT BENÉT AWARD

This award of $50 was established in 1944 in memory of the

[73]

American poet and prose writer. It is offered for a radio play in prose or verse, preferably on an American theme. It is given every two years, alternating with the Alden Award.

1944   "*T. M. D.*", by Edwin Gross.
1946   *As Sound as a Bell*, by Malvin Wald.

ETHEREGE AWARD

This competition, established in 1939, is named in honor of the great English comic writer. The prize of $100 is given for a full-length comedy. After 1945, alternates with Miles McKinnon Anderson award.

1939   *Molehills*, by Muriel Roy Bolton.
1940   *Formula for Pancakes*, by Muriel Roy Bolton.
       No Boots in Bed, by Ronald Elwy Mitchell.
1941   *Cardinal Virtue*, by Carter Kissell.
1942   *Hoe Corn, Dig 'Taters*, by Gladys Charles.
1943   No award.
1944   *The Wives of St. Joseph*, by Ronald Elwy Mitchell.
1945   *Father Was President*, by Malvin Wald and Walter Doniger.

HENRY DAVID GRAY AWARD

This contest was established in 1939 in honor of Henry David Gray, critic, scholar and playwright. It offers a prize of $50 for a piece of dramatic criticism and is designed to support interest in sound critical analysis.

1939   *Carolina Play-Making*, by William Peery.
1940   *For Mr. Shaw at Twenty-Two*, by Wanda Willson Whitman.
1941   *The Tragic Lament*, by Sherna Vinograd.
1942   *Freudian Elements in the Work of Lenormand*, by Thomas Patten Carpenter.
1943   *The Role of the Commentator in Drama*, by Miriam Goldeen.
1944   *A Generation of Still-Breeding Thoughts*, by Sr. Mary Humiliata.
1945   No award.
1946   *Wanted: Voices in the Wilderness*, by Elizabeth McCoy.

THOMAS WOOD STEVENS AWARD

This award of $100 was established in 1943 in memory of the eminent director and teacher who made history at Stanford University during his service there from 1937-39. The prize is offered for a full-length prose drama and alternates with the Maxwell Anderson Prize for verse drama.

1943   *The Shoemaker's House*, by Ronald Elwy Mitchell.
1945   *The Daylight Grows*, by Geneva Harrison.

MOTION PICTURE PRIZES

Columbia Pictures

See Prize Contests Open, Crowell's United Services Book contest, page 109.

Metro-Goldwyn-Mayer Novel Award

In 1944 Metro-Goldwyn-Mayer offered an annual novel award "for a novel considered most outstanding by a distinguished board of judges." The prize is a minimum of $125,000 to the author (maximum $175,000, contingent upon sales of the book by the publisher) and $25,000 to the publisher upon publication of the book. M-G-M reserves the motion picture and allied rights to the book. The competition is open to any unpublished but completed novel which is under contract to a United States publisher at his expense on a royalty basis.

1944 *Green Dolphin Street*, by Elizabeth Goudge. (Coward-McCann.)
1945 *Before the Sun Goes Down*, by Elizabeth Metzger Howard. (Doubleday.)
1946 *Return to Night*, by Mary Renault. (Morrow.)

Twentieth Century-Fox

See Publisher's Prizes, Doubleday New Writers Contest, page 44; Fellowships Open, Farrar, Straus Fellowship Awards, page 113.

SHORT STORY PRIZES

"Atlantic Firsts"

See Publishers' Prize, page 38.

O. Henry Memorial Award

The most important annual award in the field of short story writing is that given by the O. Henry Memorial Award committee. There are four monetary prizes and the prize-winning stories, together with others selected by the committee, are published in the yearly volumes of *O. Henry Memorial Award Prize Stories* (Doubleday). First, second and third prizes, amounting to $300, $200 and $100 respectively, are awarded to the three best stories by American authors published in American periodicals and a special prize of $100 for a first published story has been given since 1941. Earlier volumes of the series, which began in 1919, were edited by Blanche Colton Williams and Harry Hansen. The current editor is Herschel Brickell, assisted by Muriel Fuller. Since material eligible for consideration by the committee is all available in its published form, no special entry form is necessary.

1938 *The Happiest Man on Earth,* by Albert Maltz. First prize.
Fire and Cloud, by Richard Wright. Second prize.
The Promise, by John Steinbeck, Third prize.

1939 *Barn Burning,* by William Faulkner. First prize.
Bat Flight, by James Still. Second prize.
Calves, by David Cornel DeJong. Third prize.

1940 *Freedom's a Hard-Bought Thing,* by Stephen Vincent Benét. First prize.
Don't Get Me Wrong, by Roderick Lull. Second prize.
The Kill, by Edward Havill. Third prize.

1941 *Defeat,* by Kay Boyle. First prize.
A Worn Path, by Eudora Welty. Second prize.
Eighteenth Summer, by Hallie Southgate Abbett. Third prize.
The Visit, by Andy Logan. Special prize for a first published story.

1942 *The Wide Net,* by Eudora Welty. First prize.
Two Rivers, by Wallace Stegner. Second prize.
Windwagon Smith, by William L. Schramm. Third prize.
A Long Way to Go, by Jeanne E. Wylie. Special prize for a first published story.

1943 *Livvie Is Back,* by Eudora Welty. First prize.
The Knot Hole, by Dorothy Canfield. Second prize.
The Fisherman of Patzcuaro, by William Fifield. Third prize.
The Little Black Boys, by Clara Laidlaw. Special prize for a first published story.

1944 *Walking Wounded,* by Irwin Shaw. First prize.
Home Is a Place, by Bessie Breuer. Second prize.
The Stagecoach, by Griffith Beems. Third prize.
Health Card, by Frank Yerby. Special prize for a first published story.

1945 *The Wind and the Snow of Winter,* by Walter Van Tilburg Clark. First prize.
Gunners' Passage, by Irwin Shaw. Second prize.
Old Bill Bent to Drink, by Ben Hur Lampman. Third prize.
Flesh and Blood, by Laurence Critchell. Special prize for a first published story.

1946 *Bird Song,* by John Mayo Goss. First prize.
The Innocent Bystander, by Margaret Shedd. Second prize.
Sometimes You Break Even, by Victor Ullman. Third prize.
Waves of Darkness, by Cord Meyer, Jr. Special prize for a first published story.

Ellery Queen's Mystery Magazine Short Story Awards

Ellery Queen's Mystery Magazine announced in 1945 an annual $5,000 contest for detective and crime short stories. The stories must be between 5,000 and 10,000 words, by either new or established authors. The non-winners which the editor, Ellery Queen, considers acceptable will be published at the usual rates. Christopher Morley and Howard Haycraft are the other two judges. The contest is open to anyone except employees of the magazine and their families. The 1946 competition, conducted in cooperation with Little, Brown, offers prizes totalling $6,000, with a first prize of $3,000. Complete details may be obtained from Ellery Queen's Mystery Magazine, 570 Lexington Avenue, New York 22, N. Y.

1945 *A Star for a Warrior,* by Manley Wade Wellman.

BRITISH EMPIRE PRIZES

BRITAIN

Atlantic Awards in Literature

The Atlantic Awards are made from the £12,500 Rockefeller Fund which was instituted to help English writers whose creative activity was interrupted by the war. The original prize of £250 has been increased to £300. According to provisions of the Fund, similar awards will be made every year for three years. The Chairman of the committee of judges is Professor Allardyce Nicoll of Birmingham University.

1946 John Buxton, William Frank Dudley, Robert Kee, Colin Morris, Leslie Allen Paul, George Scott-Moncrieff, Arthur Teece, C. A. M. West, Laurence Whistler, Margaret Elizabeth Willy, P. H. Newby.

James Tait Black Memorial Prizes

These literary prizes, the most valuable in Great Britain, were founded by the late Mrs. Janet Coats Black in memory of her husband, a partner in the publishing house of A. and C. Black, Ltd., London. Mrs. Black set aside the sum of £11,000 to be used for two prizes of whatever income the fund should produce after paying expenses, including a fee of £50 to the judge. The prizes now amount annually to approximately £250 each. The awards are announced in the spring for books of the preceding year. The James Tait Black Memorial prizes are judged by one man, the Professor of English Literature at the University of Edinburgh, or, failing him, the Professor of English at the University of Glasgow. The judge is assisted by a staff of readers. The prizes are given for the best biography of the year and for the best work of fiction.

1919 Biography: *Samuel Butler*, by Henry Festing Jones. (Macmillan.)
      Fiction: *The Secret City*, by Hugh Walpole. (Macmillan.)
1920 Biography: *Lord Grey of the Reform Bill*, by George Macaulay Trevelyan. (Longmans.)
      Fiction: *The Lost Girl*, by D. H. Lawrence. (Viking.)
1921 Biography: *Queen Victoria*, by Lytton Strachey. (Harcourt.)
      Fiction: *Memoirs of a Midget*, by Walter de la Mare. (Knopf.)
1922 Biography: *Earlham*, by Percy Lubbock. (Scribner.)
      Fiction: *Lady into Fox*, by David Garnett. (Knopf.)
1923 Biography. *Memoirs*, by Sir Ronald Ross. (Dutton.)
      Fiction: *Riceyman Steps*, by Arnold Bennett. (Doran.)
1924 Biography: *The House of Airlie*, by Rev. William Wilson. (Murray.)

LITERARY PRIZES

	Fiction:	*A Passage to India,* by E. M. Forster. (Harcourt.)
1925	Biography:	*The Portrait of Zélide,* by Geoffrey Scott. (Scribner.)
	Fiction:	*The Informer,* by Liam O'Flaherty. (Knopf.)
1926	Biography:	*John Wyclif,* by H. B. Workman. (Oxford.)
	Fiction:	*Adam's Breed,* by Radclyffe Hall. (Houghton.)
1927	Biography:	*James Bryce,* by H. A. L. Fisher. (Macmillan.)
	Fiction:	*Love Is Enough,* by Francis Brett Young. (Knopf.) (English title: *The Portrait of Clare.*)
1928	Biography:	*Montrose,* by John Buchan. (Houghton.)
	Fiction:	*Memoirs of a Fox-Hunting Man,* by Siegfried Sassoon. (Coward-McCann.)
1929	Biography:	*The Stricken Deer,* by Lord David Cecil. (Bobbs.)
	Fiction:	*The Good Companions,* by John Boynton Priestley. (Harper.)
1930	Biography:	*Lives of a Bengal Lancer,* by Francis Yeats-Brown. (Viking.)
	Fiction:	*Miss Mole,* by E. H. Young. (Harcourt.)
1931	Biography:	*David Hume,* by J. Y. T. Grieg. (Oxford.)
	Fiction:	*Without My Cloak,* by Kate O'Brien. (Doubleday.)
1932	Biography:	*The Life of Mary Kingsley,* by Stephen Gwynn. (Macmillan.)
	Fiction:	*Boomerang,* by Helen Simpson. (Doubleday.)
1933	Biography:	*The Book of Talbot,* by Violet Clifton. (Harcourt.)
	Fiction:	*England, Their England,* by A. G. Macdonell. (Macmillan.)
1934	Biography:	*Thomas More,* by Raymond W. Chambers. (Harcourt.)
	Fiction:	*The Root and the Flower,* by L. H. Myers. (Harcourt.)
1935	Biography:	*Queen Elizabeth,* by J. E. Neale. (Harcourt.)
	Fiction:	*I, Claudius* and *Claudius the God,* by Robert Graves. (Harrison Smith.)
1936	Biography:	*Flame in Sunlight; The Life and Work of Thomas DeQuincey,* by Edward Sackville-West. (Yale.)
	Fiction:	*South Riding,* by Winifred Holtby. (Macmillan.)
1937	Biography:	*John Knox,* by Lord Eustace Percy. (Hodder.)
	Fiction:	*Highland River,* by Neil M. Gunn. (Lippincott.)
1938	Biography:	*Samuel Taylor Coleridge,* by Sir Edmund K. Chambers. (Oxford.)
	Fiction:	*Ship of the Line* and *Flying Colors,* by C. S. Forester. (Included in *Captain Horatio Hornblower.*) (Little.)
1939	Biography:	*English Scholars,* by David C. Douglas. (Transatlantic Arts.)
	Fiction:	*After Many a Summer Dies the Swan,* by Aldous Huxley. (Harper.)
1940	Biography:	*Spanish Tudor: The Life of Bloody Mary,* by Hilda F. M. Prescott. (Columbia Univ. Press.)
	Fiction:	*The Voyage,* by Charles Morgan. (Macmillan.)
1941	Biography:	*King George V,* by John Gore. (Scribner.)
	Fiction:	*A House of Children,* by Joyce Cary. (Michael Joseph.)
1942	Biography:	*Henry Ponsonby: Queen Victoria's Private Secretary,* by Arthur Ponsonby. (Macmillan.)

Fiction: *Monkey,* translated by Arthur Waley from Wu Ch'êng-ên. (John Day.)

1943 Biography: *Fourscore Years,* by Dr. G. G. Coulton. (Macmillan.)
Fiction: *Tales from Bective Bridge,* by Mary Lavin. (Little.)

1944 Biography: *William the Silent,* by Cecily V. Wedgewood. (Yale.)
Fiction: *Young Tom,* by Forrest Reid. (Faber.)

1945 Biography: *Philip Wilson Steer,* by D. S. MacColl. (Faber.)
Fiction: *Travellers,* by L. A. G. Strong. (Methuen.)

The Carnegie Medal

The Carnegie Medal is the English equivalent of the Newbery Medal awarded in America. The Carnegie Medal is given annually by the Library Association of England, in memory of Andrew Carnegie, to an outstanding book for children by a British author published in England during the preceding year.

1937 *Pigeon Post,* by Arthur Ransome. (Lippincott.)
1938 *The Family from One-End Street,* by Eve Garnett. (Vanguard.)
1939 *Circus Shoes,* by Noel Streatfield. (Random.) (English title: *The Circus Is Coming.*)
1940 *Radium Woman,* by Eleanor Doorly. (Heinemann.)
1941 *Visitors from London,* by Kitty Barne. (Dodd.)
1942 *Left Till Called For,* by Mary Treadway. (Doubleday.) (English title: *We Couldn't Leave Dinah.*)
1943 *The Little Grey Men,* by D. J. Watkins-Pitchford. (Eyre and Spottiswoode.)
1944 No award.
1945 *Wind on the Moon,* by E. Linklater. (Macmillan.)
1946 No award.

Rose Mary Crawshay Prize for English Literature

This prize was founded in 1888 in a bequest from the late Rose Mary Crawshay. Originally it was an annual prize of £100 for a work on Byron, Shelly, or Keats by an Englishwoman. In 1915 the rules were changed extending the prize to a woman of an nationality who, in the judgment of the Council of the British Academy, has written or published, within three calendar years preceding the date of the award, an historical or critical work of value on any subject concerning English literature. Preference continues to be given to works on Byron, Shelley, or Keats. The prize now may or may not be awarded annually. Information concerning this award may be obtained from the Secretary of the British Academy, Burlington Gardens, London, W. 1.

1939 No award.
1940 *Jane Austen and Her Art,* by Mary M. Lascelles. (Oxford.)

1941 *Shelley in America in the Nineteenth Century,* by Julia Power. (Univ. of Neb.)

1942 *Strolling Players and Drama in the Provinces, 1660-1765,* by Sybil Rosenfeld. (Macmillan.)

1943 *Poems of Michael Drayton,* edited by Kathleen Tillotson. (Blackwell.)

1944 *Thraliana,* by Katharine Canby Balderston. (Oxford.)

1945 *The Correspondence of Richard Steele,* by Rae Blanchard. (Oxford.)

Eyre and Spottiswoode Fellowships

Eyre and Spottiswoode, in conjunction with Houghton Mifflin, announced in 1946 an annual fellowship for British writers. This fellowship, of £1,000, is offered to young authors embarking on a literary career or established authors wishing to engage in work requiring serious study. Both fiction and non-fiction will be considered. Manuscripts submitted should be designed for the general reader, the publishers are not interested in books of a purely technical character or limited appeal. The winning books will be published in both Britain and the United States. The competition closes December 31, 1946. Complete information may be obtained from Eyre and Spottiswoode, Ltd., 14-16 Bedford Street, London, W. C. 2.

Sir Israel Gollancz Memorial Prize

This prize carries a cash award of £100 and is given biennially in memory of Sir Israel Gollancz "for published work of sufficient value on any subject connected with Old English or Early English Language and Literature, or for original investigation connected with the history of English literature or the works of English writers, with preference for the earlier period." Further information may be obtained from the British Academy, Burlington Gardens, London, W. 1.

1939 *The Text of the Canterbury Tales,* by John M. Manly and Edith Rickert. (Univ. of Chicago.)

1941 *General Work on Liturgical Drama,* by Karl Young.

1943 No award.

1945 No award.

The Greenwood Prize

The Shirley Carter Greenwood Prize, conducted under the auspices of the Poetry Society of England, is given annually for the most outstanding poem of the year. The award amounts to approximately twenty pounds.

1945 *Behold the Jew,* by A. P. Jackson. (Macmillan.)

Hawthornden Prize

The Hawthornden Prize, founded in 1919 by Alice Warrender, is a prize of £100 and a silver medal awarded annually in June to an English writer under forty-one years of age for the best work of imaginative literature. It is especially designed to encourage young authors and the word "imaginative" is given a broad interpretation — biographies are not necessarily excluded. Books do not have to be specially submitted for the prize. It is awarded without competition.

1919 *The Queen of China,* by Edward Shanks. (Knopf.)
1920 *Poems New and Old,* by John Freeman. (Harcourt.)
1921 *The Death of Society,* by Romer Wilson. (Doubleday.)
1922 *The Shepherd,* by Edmund Blunden. (Knopf.)
1923 *Lady Into Fox,* by David Garnett. (Knopf.)
1924 *The Spanish Farm,* by Ralph Hale Mottram. (Dial.)
1925 *Juno and the Paycock,* by Sean O'Casey. (Macmillan.)
1926 *The Land,* by Victoria Sackville-West. (Doubleday.)
1927 *Tarka, the Otter,* by Henry Williamson. (Dutton.)
1928 *Memoirs of a Fox-Hunting Man,* by Siegfried Sassoon. (Coward-McCann.)
1929 *The Stricken Deer,* by Lord David Cecil. (Bobbs.)
1930 *The End of the World,* by Geoffrey Dennis. (Simon & Schuster.)
1931 *Without My Cloak,* by Kate O'Brien. (Doubleday.)
1932 *The Fountain,* by Charles Morgan. (Knopf.)
1933 *Collected Poems,* by Victoria Sackville-West. (Doubleday.)
1934 *Lost Horizon,* by James Hilton. (Morrow.)
1935 *I, Claudius,* by Robert Graves. (Harrison Smith.)
1936 *Edmund Campion,* by Evelyn Waugh. (Little.)
1937 *A Trophy of Arms,* by Ruth Pitter. (Macmillan.)
1938 *In Parenthesis,* by David Michael Jones. (Faber.)
1939 *Penthesperon,* by Christopher Hassall. (Heinemann.)
1940 *London Fabric,* by James Pope-Hennessy. (Scribner.)
1941 *The Labyrinthine Ways,* by Graham Greene. (Viking.) (English title: *The Power and the Glory.*)
1942 *England Is My Village,* by John Llewelyn Rhys. (Reynal & Hitchcock.)
1943 *The Cruel Solstice* and *The Iron Laurel,* by Sidney Keyes. (Routledge.)
1944 *Letters to Malaya,* by Martyn Skinner. (Putnam.)

Heinemann Foundation for Literature Award

For many years the Heinemann (Northcliffe) Prize was offered as a reciprocal gesture to the Prix *Fémina-Vie Heureuse* Anglais. Established in 1921 by Lady Northcliffe, wife of the owner of the London *Times,* this award of £40 was offered annually for a French work of imagination worthy of representing current French letters abroad. After the death of Lord Northcliffe in 1923, there were various donors of the prize until 1934 when the firm of William Heinemann, Ltd., of London, assumed responsibility for the presentation and changed the name to the Heinemann Prize. This prize was discontinued before World War II. The Heinemann Foundation for Literature Award is a new prize, established in 1944.

The Foundation was established through a bequest in the will of the late William Heinemann, eminent British publisher. The Royal Society of Literature administers the trust which is "to encourage the production of literary works of real worth." The rules for the administration provide that no prize shall exceed the sum of £200 and that the Society is empowered to award or withhold prizes. Publishers will be invited to submit works in proof form as well as recently published books, but individual authors are not eligible to offer their work for the award.

1945 *Five Rivers,* by Norman Nicholson. (Dutton.)
1946 *Prospect of Flowers,* by Andrew Young. (Cape.)
 In Search of Two Characters, by Dormer Creston. (Scribner.)

The King's Gold Medal for Poetry

The King's Gold Medal for Poetry is offered once in three years, though not always awarded, by His Majesty the King, for a volume of poetry in English, by a British subject, published in the Empire. It is given for a poet's first or second book or to a poet under thirty-five years of age. It was instituted by King George V in 1934 and was continued by King George VI, but was suspended during the war years.

1934 *Four Walls,* by Laurence Whistler. (Macmillan.)
1937 *On This Island,* by Wystan Hugh Auden. (Random.)
1940 *Milton Blind,* by Michael Thwaites. (Blackwell.)

BRITISH EMPIRE PRIZES

The Newdigate Prize

The Newdigate Prize Foundation was established by Sir Roger Newdigate, who had been a member of Parliament for Oxford University from 1750 to 1780. This Foundation has the distinction of being the first one founded for the awarding of a literary prize. The sum of £1,000 was bequeathed by Sir Roger with directions that £21 of the income should be awarded each year to a member of Oxford University for "a copy of English verse of fifty lines and no more, in recommendation of the study of the ancient Greek and Roman remains of architecture, sculpture, and painting." Later, with the consent of the Newdigate heirs, the strict conditions governing the competition were changed.

No woman had ever won the Newdigate Prize until the year 1927, when Miss Gertrude Trevelyan had the distinction of being the first woman recipient. Since then this most famous of undergraduate prizes has been awarded to two other women. Among the recipients of the prize who later attained great distinction in the field of literature are such names as John Ruskin, Matthew Arnold, Dean Stanley, Oscar Wilde, John Buchan, Julian Huxley.

There has been no Newdigate Prize award since the outbreak of war in 1939.

1935 *Canterbury,* by Allan W. Plowman. (Blackwell.)
1936 *Rain,* by D. M. de R. Winser. (Blackwell.)
1937 *The Man in the Moon,* by Margaret Stanley-Wrench. (Blackwell.)
1938 *Milton Blind,* by Michael Thwaites. (Blackwell.)
1939 *Dr. Newman Revisits Oxford,* by Kenneth S. Kitchin. (Blackwell.)

The John Llewelyn Rhys Memorial Prize

The John Llewelyn Rhys Memorial Prize was established in 1941 from a trust left by this young airman, who was posthumously awarded the Hawthornden Prize for his book of short stories, *England Is My Village.* The prize is awarded annually to a man or woman under thirty, a citizen of the British Empire, for a memorable work, either "in achievement or in promise." Entries must have been published for the first time during the previous calendar year and may be fiction, non-fiction, poetry or drama. The announcement of the award is usually made in June. Further information concerning the award may be obtained by writing to 23 Maida Avenue, London, W. 2.

1942 *Sunk by a Mine,* by Michael Richey. (New York Times Magazine.)

1943 *Beauty for Ashes,* by Morwenna Donelly. (Routledge.)
1944 *The Last Inspection,* by Alun Lewis. (Posthumous award.)
      (Macmillan.)
1945 *The Sea Eagle,* by James Aldridge. (Little.)
1946 *My Bird Sings,* by Oriel Malet. (Faber.)

Sunday Times Literary Prize

In 1946 the London *Sunday Times* inaugurated an annual prize of £1,000 for a book that makes an "outstanding contribution to English literature." In addition to the monetary award, the author of the winning book will receive a commemorative gold medal. The prize will be given for a work by a British subject published. during the twelve months, ending June 30, preceding the award. The initial award will be given for a book published for the first time during the period from July 1, 1946 to June 30, 1947.

AUSTRALIA

S. H. Prior Memorial Prize

The S. H. Prior Memorial Prize was established in 1934 in recognition of the services to Australian literature of Samuel Henry Prior, for many years the editor of *The Sydney Bulletin.* An annual award is given by his son, H. K. Prior, for the most outstanding contribution of the year to Australian literature. Before the war the award amounted to £500 (Australian), but has now been reduced to £100. Any literary work by an Australian author is eligible and, for the purposes of this award, this includes residents of Australia and New Zealand. The *Bulletin* reserves the right to publish the winning book in serial form, but all other publishing rights belong to the author. No work that has already won a monetary prize is eligible. Full details of the contest can be obtained from the Trustees, S. H. Prior Memorial Prize, Bulletin Office, 252 George Street, Sydney, Australia.

1935   *Tiburon,* by Kylie Tennant. (Endeavor.)
1936   *All that Swagger,* by Miles Franklin. (Bulletin.)
1937   No award.
1938   No award.
1939   *Who Was Joseph Furphy?,* by Miles Franklin. (Angus.)
1940   *The Pea-Pickers,* by Eve Langley. (Published in America, 1946, as *Not Yet The Moon,* Dutton.)
       The Battlers, by Kylie Tennant. (Macmillan.)
       Lachlan Macquarie, by M. H. Ellis.
1941   *It's Harder for Girls,* by Gavin Casey. (Angus.)
1942   No award.
1943   No award.
1944   No award.
1945   *The Fire on the Snow,* by Douglas Stewart. (Angus.)
1946   *Cookabundy Bridge,* by Brian James.

CANADA

Governor-General's Literary Awards

The Governor-General's Literary Awards were first given in 1937, for books published during the preceding year. The awards were established by John Buchan, Lord Tweedsmuir, then Governor-General of Canada, as a permanent system of recognition for literary merit. All necessary arrangements, including the selection of judges and the making of rules, are entrusted to the Canadian Authors' Association. The awards take the form of bronze medals and are presented to the authors of the best books in four classes—poetry, fiction, academic non-fiction and creative non-fiction—published each calendar year. The authors must be residents of Canada. For more detailed information, inquire of the Canadian Authors' Association, William Arthur Deacon, 66 Parkhurst Blvd., Toronto 12, Canada.

FICTION

1937	*Think of the Earth,* by Bertram B. Brooker. (Nelson.)
1938	*The Dark Weaver,* by Laura G. Salverson. (Ryerson.)
1939	*Swiss Sonata,* by Gwethalyn Graham. (Nelson.)
1940	*The Champlain Road,* by Franklin D. McDowell. (Macmillan.)
1941	*Thirty Acres,* by Ringuet. (Macmillan.)
1942	*Three Came to Ville Marie,* by Alan Sullivan. (Coward, McCann.)
1943	*Little Man,* by Herbert Sallans. (Humphries.)
1944	*The Pied Piper of Dipper Creek,* by Thomas H. Raddall. (McClelland.)
1945	*Earth and High Heaven,* by Gwethalyn Graham. (Lippincott.)
1946	*Two Solitudes,* by Hugh MacLennan. (Duell.)

NON-FICTION

(From 1937 to 1942 one award was given in the field of General Literature. Since that time two awards have been given in the non-fiction field, one for creative non-fiction and one for academic non-fiction.)

1937	*Newspaper Pieces,* by T. B. Robertson. (Macmillan.)
1938	*My Discovery of the West,* by Stephen Leacock. (Hale.)
1939	*Canadian Mosaic,* by J. M. Gibbon. (Dodd.)
1940	*Confessions of an Immigrant's Daughter,* by Laura G. Salverson. (Ryerson.)
1941	*Slava Bohu,* by J. F. C. Wright. (Nelson.)
1942	*Klee Wyck,* by Emily Carr. (Farrar & Rinehart.)

BRITISH EMPIRE PRIZES

1943 *The Unknown Country*, by Bruce Hutchison. (Coward, McCann.)
The Unguarded Frontier, by Edgar McInnis. (Doubleday.)
1944 *The Incomplete Anglers*, by John D. Robins. (Duell.)
On Canadian Poetry, by E. K. Brown. (Ryerson.)
1945 *Partner in Three Worlds*, by Dorothy Duncan. (Harper.)
The War: Fourth Year, by Edgar McInnis. (Oxford.)
1946 *Gauntlet to Overlord*, by Ross Munro. (Macmillan.)
We Keep a Light, by Evelyn Fox Richardson. (Ryerson.)

POETRY

1937 No award.
1938 *The Fable of the Goats*, by E. J. Pratt. (Macmillan.)
1939 *By Stubborn Stars*, by Kenneth Leslie. Humphries.)
1940 *Under the Sun*, by Arthur S. Bourinot. (Macmillan.)
1941 *Brebeuf and His Brethren*, by E. J. Pratt. (Macmillan.)
1942 *Calling Adventurers*, by Anne Marriott. (Ryerson.)
1943 *David and Other Poems*, by Earle Birney. (Ryerson.)
1944 *News of the Phoenix*, by A. J. M. Smith. (Coward, McCann.)
1945 *Day and Night*, by Dorothy Livesay. (Ryerson.)
1946 *Now Is Time*, by Earle Birney. (Ryerson.)

Leacock Medal for Humor

The Leacock Memorial Committee established this annual award in 1946. The Medal will be awarded for the best Canadian book of humor of each calendar year. The first presentation will be made for books published during 1946. The judging will be done under the Governor-General's Awards Board, but the presentation will be separate. The Public Library of Orillia, Ontario is the trustee for the award. Further information may be obtained from William Arthur Deacon, 66 Parkhurst Blvd., Toronto 12, Canada.

Longmans, Green—Coward-McCann Prize Contest

In June 1943, Coward-McCann, Inc. of New York and Longmans, Green and Company of Toronto offered a joint prize of $1,000 for the best book of fiction or non-fiction by a Canadian citizen living in Canada or serving in the Canadian forces outside Canada. The contest, with a prize of $1,000 in addition to royalties, was open to books on any subject, in English, or translated from French into English.

1944 *Darkly the River Flows*, by John Macdonald. (Coward-McCann.)

LITERARY PRIZES

The Ryerson Fiction Award

The Ryerson Press of Toronto offers this award to a Canadian author for a manuscript of merit. The manuscripts are judged by a representative of the Ryerson Press and a representative of the Canadian Authors' Association. The prize of $1,000 is given half as an outright prize and half on account of royalties. The competition was inaugurated to encourage native Canadian writers. The only restriction on subject matter is that spy, detective and crime stories are ineligible. Details may be obtained from the Ryerson Press, 299 Queen Street West, Toronto 2B, Canada.

1942 *Little Man,* by Herbert Sallans.
1943 No award.
1944 No award.
1945 *Day of Wrath,* by Philip Child.
Here Stays Good Yorkshire, by Will R. Bird.
1946 No award.

Royal Society of Canada Medal Awards

The Royal Society of Canada awards five medals, two of which are of particular interest to the literary world, the other three being for scientific achievement. These medals are usually awarded annually, but not necessarily so, if, in the opinion of the committee in charge, no person has made a contribution worthy of such honor. The Lorne Pierce Medal is given for accomplishments in imaginative or critical literature and the Tyrrell Medal for outstanding work in connection with the history of Canada. The other three are the Flavelle Medal, established in 1925, for original research in the biological sciences; the Henry Marshall Tory Medal, established in 1943, for outstanding contributions to some branch of physics, chemistry, mathematics, astronomy, or allied sciences; and the Willet G. Miller Medal, also established in 1943, to North American residents who have completed and published outstanding research in geology, mineralogy, or allied sciences. For complete details, address the Royal Society of Canada, National Research Building, Ottowa, Ontario, Canada.

BRITISH EMPIRE PRIZES

THE LORNE PIERCE MEDAL

This medal is the gift of Dr. Lorne Pierce of Toronto, and is awarded to Fellows of the Royal Society of Canada, or others who are Canadian citizens, for achievement of special significance and conspicuous merit in imaginative or critical literature. Works may be in French or English, with preference to Canadian subjects. Previous winners of this award can be found in the 1939 edition of *Famous Literary Prizes and Their Winners*.

1939 Wilfred Bovey.
1940 E. J. Pratt.
1941 Leon Gerin.
1942 Watson Kirkconnell.
1943 George H. Clarke.
1944 Audrey Alexandra Brown.
1945 L'Abbé Félix-Antoine Savard.
1946 Charles N. Cochrane.

TYRRELL MEDAL

The Tyrrell Medal is the gift of J. B. Tyrrell of Toronto, and is awarded by the Royal Society of Canada for research work in Canadian history, in French or English, whether published or not, and may include works of biography and the collection of historical material. Preference is given to a Canadian citizen, but the winner is not necessarily a Canadian. Previous winners of this award can be found in the 1939 edition of *Famous Literary Prizes and Their Winners*.

1939 E.-Z. Massicotte.
1940 Chester Martin.
1941 Arthur S. Morton.
1942 D. C. Harvey.
1943 Gustave Lanctot.
1944 Harold A. Innis.
1945 Fred Landon.
1946 A. L. Burt

NEW ZEALAND

Esther Glen Award

At its annual conference early in 1945, the New Zealand Library Association announced the establishment of an award to be made each year to the author of the most distinguished contribution to New Zealand literature for children. The award is named in honor of Esther Glen, New Zealand author and editor of the children's page in the Christchurch *Sun*. The first award was made during Book Week in November 1945

1945 *The Book of Wiremu,* by Stella Morice. (Paul's Book Arcade.)

CONTINENTAL PRIZES

CZECHOSLOVAKIA

Czechoslovak State Prize

The Czechoslovak State Prizes have been awarded annually since 1920 on October twenty-eighth, Czechoslovak Independence Day, for the most outstanding works of the year in many artistic fields. The State Prizes are given for literary works—poetry, fiction, essays, drama—for stage productions, outstanding acting, operatic works, musical compositions, musical performances, as well as for films, painting and sculpture. The best-known and finest Czechoslovak writers were former recipients of the literature prizes—Karel Capek, Josef Capek, Vladislav Vancura, to mention but a few. During the war the government-in-exile, anxious to further the artistic, musical and literary life of its people abroad and to encourage the friends of its people in other countries who interpret Czechoslovak creative achievements and traditions, continued the award. The prize, formerly in money (5,000 crowns), now takes the form of a small bronze bust of T. G. Masaryk.

In 1945, in place of the awards, Dr. Zdenek Nejedly, Minister of Education and Culture, published a decree paying tribute to the Czechoslovak artists and scientists who were killed fighting their oppressors and to those who died in prison camps. This roster included over a hundred names in the fields of literature, music, theater, creative art and architecture, and science.

1940 *Czechoslovakia: Twenty Years of Independence,* by Robert J. Kerner. (Univ. of Calif. Press.)
1941 *To Sing with the Angels* and *We Shall Live Again,* by Maurice Hindus. (Doubleday.)
1942 No award.
1943 *Czechoslovakia in European History,* by Dr. S. Harrison Thomson. (Princeton Univ. Press.)
1944 No award.
1945 See above.

FRANCE

French Academy Prizes

The literary prizes awarded annually by the French Academy total one hundred and fifty in number, a list too extensive to be included here. The Novel Prize has always been the one attracting most attention and the winning book has often been translated into English. The Grand Prize for Literature amounts to 10,000 francs, the largest monetary award given by the Academy. The Academy was founded in the seventeenth century and its prizes have been given for many years.

GRAND PRIZE FOR LITERATURE

This annual prize of 10,000 francs is given by the French Academy to a writer of prose or to a poet for either a single work or for many works of high inspiration and distinguished style. The prize may not be divided. If, in any year, the prize is not awarded, the sum is used to increase the endowment of other Academy prizes.

1919	Jérôme and Jean Tharaud.	1933	Henri Duvernois.
1920	Edmond Jaloux.	1934	Henry de Montherlant.
1921	Comtesse de Noailles.	1935	André Suares.
1922	Pierre Lasserre.	1936	Pierre Camo.
1923	François Porché.	1937	Maurice Magre.
1924	Abel Bonnard.	1938	Tristan Derème.
1925	General Mangin.	1939	Jacques Boulenger.
1926	Gilbert de Voisins.	1940	Edmond Pilon.
1927	Joseph de Pesquidoux.	1941	Gabriel Faure.
1928	Jean-Louis Vaudoyer.	1942	Jean Schlumberger.
1929	Henri Massis.	1943	Jean Prévost.
1930	Marie-Louise Pailleron.	1944	André Billy.
1931	Raymond Escholier.	1945	Jean Paulhan.
1932	Franc-Nohain.	1946	Henry Daniel-Rops.

NOVEL PRIZE

This annual prize of 5,000 francs is given by the French Academy to a young writer of prose for a work of imagination and high inspiration. If not awarded in any year, the amount is to be carried over to the next year when two prizes may be awarded. Any unused amount is used to increase the endowment of open competitions in prose.

1919	Pierre Benoit.	1921	Pierre Villetard.
1920	Madame André Corthis.	1922	Francis Carco.

1923	Alphonse de Châteaubriant.	1935	Albert Touchard.
1924	Emile Henriot.	1936	Georges Bernanos.
1925	François Duhourcan.	1937	Guy de Pourtalès.
1926	François Mauriac.	1938	Jean Mallart de la Varende.
1927	Joseph Kessel.	1939	Antoine de Saint-Exupéry.
1928	Jean Balde.	1940	Edouard Peisson.
1929	André Demaison.	1941	Robert Bourget-Pailleron.
1930	Jacques de Lacretelle.	1942	Jean Blanzat.
1931	Henri Pourrat.	1943	Joseph Henri Louwyck.
1932	T'sterstevens.	1944	Pierre Lagarde.
1933	Roger Chauviré.	1945	Marc Blancpain.
1934	Madame Paule Régnier.	1946	Orieux.

The Goncourt Prize

The Goncourt Prize of 5,000 francs has long been one of the most coveted literary prizes in France. Its annual award in December is eagerly awaited and predictions of winners are as rife as the violently dissenting opinions following the decision. The Goncourt selection of the best novel has been said to exert more influence on the literary taste and tendencies of the time than the 150 prizes of the French Academy.

The Goncourt Academy was founded by Edmond de Goncourt and his brother, Jules, who were the creators of the "impressionist" school of fiction. The Academy was to consist of ten members who were to confer an annual award of 5,000 francs upon "the best work of imagination in prose, and exclusively in prose, published during the year, which best exemplified youth, boldness and talent." After seven years of litigation the Goncourt Academy was finally organized and the first award was made in 1903.

The Goncourt Academy was founded more or less in opposition to the French Academy. The founders wanted it to represent independent literature as opposed to the "official and fashionable" authors of the French Academy. The pomposity of that sacrosanct body, who call themselves the Forty Immortals, was offset by the bohemianism of the half-score of non-conforming writers who held their meetings, not in the Mazarin Palace, but in Drouant's restaurant and who had, instead of public lectures, nothing but a monthly lunch.

The earliest award of the Goncourt Academy was made in keeping with the defiant tradition of the Goncourts. The prize was given to a novel dealing with insanity, a book unwholesome in tone and written in an extravagant style. Afterwards the

Goncourt academicians confessed their mistake in making such a freakish selection and in later years they tended to crown books that have been widely acceptable. The Goncourt Prize has always been given to a young beginner, never to an old established author.

Monsieur J. H. Rosny, Sr., former president of the Goncourt Academy, who died in 1940, published his *Mémoirs de la Vie Littéraire,* containing the history of the Goncourt Academy.

Prize winners from 1903 through 1938 may be found in the 1939 edition of *Famous Literary Prizes and Their Winners.*

1939 *Les Enfants Gâtés,* by Phillipe Hériat.
1940 *Les Grandes Vacances,* by Francis Ambrière. (Awarded in 1946. The prize money for 1940 was held until after the war, to be given to the best book by a former war prisoner or deportee.)
1941 *Vent de Mars,* by Henri Pourrat.
1942 *Pareils à des Enfants,* by Marc Bernard.
1943 *Passage de l'Homme,* by Marius Grout.
1944 No award.
1945 *Le Premier Accroc Coute 200 Francs,* by Elsa Triolet.
1946 *Mon Village à l'Heure Allemande,* by Jean-Louis Bory.

Prix Femina-Vie Heureuse

The French Prix *Fémina-Vie Heureuse* of 5,000 francs was founded in 1904 by a group of French women writers and was awarded for the best work of imagination in the French language, prose or poetry, by a man or woman. It was offered by two French periodicals, *Femina* and *La Vie Heureuse.* The list of prize winners from 1904-1938 is given in the 1939 edition of *Literary Prizes and Their Winners.*

In 1919 the *Femina* committee voted to extend their prize to foreign countries, establishing in that year the Prix *Fémina-Vie Heureuse* Anglais, later known as the Stock Prize, and in 1932 the Prix *Femina* American. Reciprocal prizes were established in England and the United States. The Heinemann (Northcliffe) Prize is described on page 86. The America-France Award was discontinued in 1936, after three awards had been made. For details see the 1939 edition of *Famous Literary Prizes and Their Winners.*

1939 *La Rose de la Mer,* by Paul Vialar.
1940-1944 No awards.
1945 *Les Editions de Minuit* (Refused the award.)
1946 *Le Chemin du Soleil,* by Ann-Marie Monnet.

PORTUGAL

The Camões Prize

This prize is given by the Portuguese government for the best literary or scientific work by a foreign author published in English, French, German, Portuguese, Spanish or Italian on the subject of "Portugal", its history, art, architecture, culture, or any other aspect of the country.

The award has a monetary value of 20,000 escudos (approximately £200 at the 1943 rate of currency exchange). It was founded as a memorial to Luis Camões, 16th century Portuguese poet. The prize is awarded biennially by a jury consisting of six Portuguese writers of recognized merit, together with the director of the Secretariado da Propaganda Nacional. The winning author is invited to visit Lisbon for personal presentation of the award. In 1946 the prize will be awarded for the years 1944 and 1945.

1937 *Portugal,* by Gonzague de Reynold.
1939 *I Gathered No Moss,* by John Gibbons. (Hale.)
1941 *La Revolución Portuguesa,* by Jesús Pabón.
1943 *Land of Prester John,* by Elaine Sanceau. (Knopf.)

SWEDEN

Swedish Novel Prize

The Ljus Publishing Company, Stockholm, in cooperation with the Thomas Y. Crowell Company, Metro-Goldwyn-Mayer and George G. Harrap and Company, Ltd., London, offered $25,000 (the largest monetary award, except for the Nobel Prize, ever offered in Scandinavia) for a novel. The contest, which closed May 1, 1946, was open only to authors writing in the Scandinavian languages and provided for book and film rights. The book will be published in Sweden, Norway, France, and the Netherlands.

1946 *In the Last Moment,* by Thore Ericsson.
    Echo of a Voice, by Nanna Lindefjeld. Extra award.

Stalin Prizes

The Stalin Prizes were instituted in 1939 by the order of the Council of the People's Commissars of the U. S. S. R. in honor of the sixtieth birthday of Joseph Stalin, and were first awarded in 1941. Over one hundred and fifty prizes are awarded annually in various fields — science, invention, music, films, medicine, theater, dance, art and literature. In 1942 eighteen first prizes of 100,000 rubles each were given in the field of art and literature.

Not all of the prize-winning books have been translated or published in the United States. Therefore, the list below includes only those which are available in translation, and is as complete as possible within this limitation.

Fall of Paris, by Ilya Ehrenburg. (Knopf.)
Taras' Family, by Boris Gorbatov. (Cattell.)
Two Captains, by Benjamin Kaverin. (Modern Age.)
The Front, by Alexander Korneichuk. (Macmillan.)
Chariot of Wrath and *Road to the Ocean,* by Leonid Leonov. (Fischer.)
      (Prize won for untranslated work.)
Twelve Months, by Samuel Marshak. (Yale.)
Pugavhev, by Anatole Shishkov. (Crowell.)
Quiet Flows the Don, by Mikhail A. Sholokhov. (Knopf.)
Days and Nights, by Konstantin Simonov. (Simon & Schuster.)
The Russian People, by Konstantin Simonov. (Macmillan.)
Soul of the Sea, by Leonid Sobolev. (Lippincott.)
Road to Calvary, by Alexei Tolstoy. (Knopf.)
The Rainbow, by Wanda Wasielewska. (Simon & Schuster.)

Further Information on Foreign Awards

Information concerning literary prizes and their winners in foreign countries may be obtained from *Books Abroad,* a publication of the University of Oklahoma Press, Norman, Oklahoma. This magazine, which reviews books published in all countries outside the United States, is published quarterly and for the past dozen years has carried annually in its Winter Number a section called "Literary Landmarks" which includes news of international prizes.

LATIN AMERICAN PRIZES

LATIN AMERICAN PRIZES

There are many literary prizes given in all of Latin America, sponsored by countries, cities, book trade associations, libraries, periodicals and publishing houses. During the past few years it has been impossible to compile accurate and complete information about these awards. The Winter Number of *Books Abroad,* published by the University of Oklahoma, Norman, Oklahoma, carries rather extensive information on the miscellaneous prizes given in Latin America.

Latin American Prize Novel Contest

Farrar and Rinehart, the Division of Intellectual Cooperation of the Pan American Union and *Redbook* Magazine announced in 1940 a prize contest for the best book, preferaby a novel, by a Latin American author. The competition, which offered a prize of $2,500, was judged by an international jury consisting of Ernesto Montenegro, Blair Niles, and John Dos Passos.

In 1943 the prizes consisted of $2,000 for the best novel, $2,000 for the best work of non-fiction, and $1,000 for the best children's book.

1941 *El Mundo es Ancho y Ajeno (Broad and Alien is the World)*, by Ciro Alegria of Chile.
1943 Fiction: *Canapé-Vert,* by Pierre Marcelin and Philippe Thoby-Marcelin of Haiti.
Non-fiction: *Peregrinaje,* by Argentina Díaz Lozando of Honduras.
Juvenile: *Lautaro: El Joven Libertador de Aranco,* by Fernando Alegría of Chile.

CONTESTS OPEN

Prize Contests Open

This list is compiled from information available in the fall of 1946 — closing dates are subject to change. A similar list appears annually in "The Literary Market Place" (Bowker) with completely up-to-date information.

Prize & Sponsor	Amount	Conditions	Closing Date
Abingdon-Cokesbury Annual Award, 150 Fifth Avenue, New York 11, N. Y.	$7,500	"A book that will accomplish the greatest good for the Christian faith and Christian living among all peoples."	February 1, 1947
Atlantic Monthly Novel Prize, 8 Arlington St., Boston 8, Mass.	$10,000	For a novel—no restrictions as to author or subject.	January 15, 1947
"*Atlantic First*" Story Award, 8 Arlington St., Boston 8, Mass.	$1,500 Second Prize of $750	Stories from 2,000 to 20,000 words by new writers, for publication in the *Atlantic Monthly*.	Awards made for best story in each six-month period.
Bross Foundation Prize, Lake Forest College, Lake Forest, Ill.	$15,000	For the best book or manuscript on the relation of any branch of knowledge to the Christian religion.	Award to be made in 1950.
Crowell's United Services Book Contest, 432 Fourth Ave., New York 16, N. Y.	$6,000	For fiction or non-fiction, open to any past or present member of the armed forces of the United Nations. Conducted in cooperation with Columbia Pictures and George G. Harrap & Co. of London.	June 30, 1947
Dodd, Mead-*Redbook* Novel Award, 230 Park Avenue, New York 17, N. Y.	$10,000	Open to any American or Canadian author who has not published more than two novels in book form or serially.	Summer, 1947
Dodd, Mead, Red Badge Contest, 432 Fourth Avenue, New York 16, N. Y.	$1,000	For a detective story by a writer who has not previously had a novel published under the Red Badge imprint.	April 1, 1947 October 1, 1947

Prize & Sponsor	Amount	Conditions	Closing Date
Doubleday, *Kenyon Review* Short Story Contest; Address Kenyon Review, Gambier, Ohio	$500 Second Prize of $250	For a short story by an author who has never published a book of fiction.	Spring, 1947
Doubleday Prize Novel Contest, 14 W. 49th St., New York 20, N. Y.	$20,000	Open to new and established writers of any nationality.	Summer, 1947
Doubleday's George Washington Carver Memorial Award, 14 W. 49th St., New York 20, N. Y.	$2,500	Fiction, non-fiction or poetry which "makes an effective contribution the Negro's place in American life."	Open
Dutton's Lewis & Clark Northwest Contest, 300 Fourth Ave., New York 10, N. Y.	$3,000	For a manuscript by a Northwest author.	February 1, 1947
Dutton's Thomas Jefferson Southern Award, 300 Fourth Ave., New York 10, N. Y.	$2,500	For a manuscript by a Southern author.	Spring, 1947
Dutton Sports Story Award 300 Fourth Ave., New York 10, N. Y.	$500	Sports editors of newspapers and magazines are invited to submit sports stories from their publications.	December, 1946
Eerdman's Evangelical Book Award, 255 Jefferson Ave., Grand Rapids, Michigan	$5,000	For a novel in the field of evangelical Christianity.	September 1, 1947
Julia Ellsworth Ford Foundation Prize, c/o Julian Messner, Inc., 8 W. 40th St., New York 18, N. Y.	$1,250	For a juvenile manuscript.	Spring, 1947

Prize & Sponsor	Amount	Conditions	Closing Date
Harper Prize Novel Competitions, 49 E. 33rd St., New York 16, N. Y.	$10,000	For an outstanding novel.	June 1, 1947
Hopwood Prizes, University of Michigan, Ann Arbor, Michigan	Awards from $75 to $2,500	Open to regularly enrolled students at the University of Michigan for novels, non-fiction, verse, drama.	Spring, 1947
Houghton Mifflin Life-in-America Awards, 2 Park St., Boston 7, Mass.	$2,500	Fiction or non-fiction "presenting a true and vivid account of life in America."	Open
Houghton Mifflin, *Southwest Review* Contest, 2 Park St., Boston 7, Mass.	$1,000	For fiction or non-fiction by an author whose work has previously appeared in the *Southwest Review*.	December 15, 1946
League to Support Poetry, 327 W. 18th St., New York, N. Y.	Publication of manuscript by the League.	For a volume of poetry.	February, 1947
Loubat Prizes, Columbia University, New York, N. Y.	$1,000 Second Prize of $400	For a published work on the history, geography, ethnology, archaeology, etc. of North America.	1948
M-G-M Novel Award, 1540 Broadway, New York, N. Y.	$125,000	For an outstanding novel under contract to a publisher.	July, 1947
Poetry Magazine, 232 E. Erie St., Chicago, Ill.	See pp. 66-68	Awards are given for work that has appeared in the magazine during the preceding year.	Announced in November issue of the magazine.

Prize & Sponsor	Amount	Conditions	Closing Date
Ellery Queen's Mystery Magazine Short Story Award, 570 Lexington Ave., New York 22, N. Y.	$5,000	For a detective or crime short story by a new or established author. Conducted in cooperation with Little, Brown.	October, 1947
Charles H. Sergel Play Contest, University of Chicago, Chicago, Ill.	$1,000	Open to any United States citizen for a full-length play.	1947
Stanford University Awards, Stanford University, Calif.	See pp. 72-74	Seven different awards in the field of drama.	February 15, 1947
Westminster Press Annual Award, 952 Witherspoon Bldg., Philadelphia 7, Penn.	$8,000	For the best novel "emphasizing the influence of Christian faith in contemporary life or history."	Spring, 1947
Yale Series of Younger Poets, Yale University Press, New Haven, Conn.	$100 plus publication of the book	Open to American citizens under thirty who have not previously published a volume of verse.	March 1, 1947

Literary Fellowships Open

For later information, see annual volumes of "The Literary Market Place" (Bowker.)

Prize & Sponsor	Amount	Conditions	Closing Date
Bruce Publishing Company Fellowships, 540 N. Michigan St., Milwaukee 1, Wis.	$1,200	Fellowships in biography and fiction, open to any Catholic lay person.	Open
Dodd, Mead Intercollegiate Literary Fellowship, 432 Fourth Avenue, New York 16, N. Y.	$1,200	Open to American college students for a novel outline.	April 1, 1947
Farrar, Straus - Twentieth Century-Fox Fellowship Awards, 580 Fifth Ave., New York 19, N. Y.	$3,500 and royalties. Total payment from film company not to exceed $150,000.	For a completed but unpublished novel by working newspaper or magazine writers. Called Journalists Fellowship Awards.	Open
Guggenheim Memorial Fellowships, 551 Fifth Avenue, New York 17, N. Y.	According to need of recipient for period of fellowship.	"To provide opportunities for men and women of high ability to further their work."	Spring, 1947
Harper's Eugene Saxton Memorial Fellowships, 49 E. 33rd St., New York 16, N. Y.	No fixed value. Not to exceed $2,500 in any one year.	To aid creative writers, especially new ones without publishing connections.	Open
Houghton Mifflin Literary Fellowship, 2 Park St., Boston 7, Mass.	$2,400	Fiction or non-fiction by promising young writers.	January, 1947
Journalists Fellowship Awards		See Farrar, Straus above.	

Prize & Sponsor	Amount	Conditions	Closing Date
Alfred A. Knopf Literary Fellowships, 501 Madison Ave., New York 22, N. Y.	American History or Biography: $5,000 & $2,500. Science: $2,500. Fiction: $2,500.	"For the purpose of assisting talented writers in completing planned, unfinished novels."	Open
Pellegrini & Cudahy Fellowships, 75 E. Wacker Drive, Chicago 1, Ill.	Three awards of $2,100 each.	Open to any writer under 36 who lives in the Middle West or to writers living outside the Middle West who are working on subjects of Middle Western interest.	March 31, 1947
Putnam Award at the William Allen White School of Public Information, University of Kansas, c/o G. P. Putnam's Sons, 2 W. 45th St., New York 19, N. Y.	$2,500	For a completed manuscript or project which meets the approval of the judges.	Spring, 1947
Simon & Schuster Fellowship Fund, 1230 Sixth Ave., N. Y.	No fixed value.	For new writers under 38.	Open
Ann Watkins Fellowships, 77 Park Avenue, New York 16, N. Y.	$1,500 & $500	To citizens of the United States under thirty years of age who are enrolled in the University of Chicago.	Summer, 1947
Whittlesey House Southwestern Fellowship Award, 330 W. 42nd St., New York, N. Y.	$2,000	Fiction or non-fiction. Manuscript must deal in some way with the four Southwestern states: Arizona, New Mexico, Oklahoma, Texas.	March 1, 1947

INDEX

[115]

INDEX

(*Continued*)

INDEX

(*Continued*)

INDEX

(*Continued*)

INDEX
(*Continued*)